Managing Sustainable Innovation

Advance Praise

"Overall, Ian Maxwell has taken a multi-national up-to-date perspective on innovation, which makes the book a useful resource in many contexts. The early chapters set the principles for thinking about innovation and its role in regional and global economic growth, in an accessible and practical way, while later chapters describe many cases of innovative technology. For example, the chapter dealing with renewable energy innovation has an immediacy which relates to the current volatility of global energy economics. *Managing Sustainable Innovation* is a valuable commentary on the essence of innovation, emerging technologies and innovative companies."

Professor Ralph Cooney
Pro Vice Chancellor (Tamaki)
The University of Auckland

"In the 21st-century world, increasingly driven by innovation, Ian's work is insightful, thoughtful, and timely. Complex issues are distilled into simple understandable concepts that are universal with broad applicability across industries, businesses, and countries. This work should be invaluable in managing research portfolios and resources, and developing an innovative culture for long-term sustainable growth and competitive advantage. A must read book for executives, leaders, educators, and professionals irrespective of the industry they are working in!"

Dr. Baljit Gambhir
Managing Consultant
Shell Global Solutions (US) Incorporated

"This book provides insight into the most up-to-date ideas and approaches to innovation that are very valuable to any organisation, commercial or governmental."

Professor Thomas Maschmeyer
ARC Federation Fellow
University of Sydney

"Ian Maxwell offers a practical approach to innovation management and highlights the importance of environmentally sustainable innovation and policy in developing countries. Applying years of research, application and enthusiasm, Dr. Maxwell includes numerous examples from high-tech, telecommunications and energy, among others."

Dr. Jan van der Eijk
Chief Technology Officer
Royal Dutch Shell
The Netherlands

Ian E. Maxwell

Managing Sustainable Innovation

The Driver for Global Growth

 Springer

Ian E. Maxwell
Maxco Consulting Group
Takapuna 0740
New Zealand
ianmaxwell@maxco.co.nz

ISBN 978-0-387-87580-4   ISBN 978-0-387-87581-1 (eBook)
DOI 10.1007/978-0-387-87581-1

Library of Congress Control Number: 2008934454

Printed on acid-free paper

springer.com

THE UNIVERSITY OF
WINCHESTER

Martial Rose Library
Tel: 01962 827306

Publisher Disclaimer

Preface

The last decade has seen an almost explosive growth of innovation both globally and across a wide range of business sectors. World class companies that have embraced innovation and have built a strong innovation infrastructure are experiencing high growth and sustainable financial performance. Many companies, however, are still struggling to develop such an infrastructure and are lagging behind in the new global innovation race.

Countries that have built both a foundation of science and technology and a strong innovation infrastructure are enjoying strong Gross Domestic Product (GDP) growth and high living standards, as measured by GDP per capita. In contrast, countries that are unable to create and sustain an innovation foundation and infrastructure will be challenged to compete and therefore increase or maintain living standards in the new knowledge-based global economy.

In this book, insights are provided into modern concepts and management tools to enhance and inspire innovation through a wide range of illustrative examples drawn from diverse business sectors such as IT, clean and renewable energy, healthcare and nanotechnology. University-driven innovation and the crucial role of venture capital in building an innovation infrastructure are discussed. In addition, the potentially disruptive low-cost innovation model emerging from countries such as China and India is addressed, along with some examples of small countries that are proactively developing a strong innovative infrastructure.

Somewhat surprisingly, the management of the innovation process is still embryonic compared with other aspects of business management, possibly due to the relatively high level of complexity. The concepts of incremental, quantum and disruptive modes of innovation are discussed, demonstrating how high-growth companies proactively manage the time to market and allocate resources to these different modes. Innovation management is divided into "soft" and "hard" management phases. The first phase involves idea generation and screening, while the second phase is much more focused on project management and "speed to market." Companies that embrace structured innovation management systems and drive a "top down" innovation culture that permeates the entire company will be most likely to achieve sustainable high growth and strong shareholder returns.

Successful innovative applications of the Internet have spawned new multi-billion dollar companies such as Google, eBay, Amazon, Facebook, Alibaba,

YouTube and Double Click. New multi-functional and web-linked devices, such as the iPhone from Apple and the Kindle e-book from Amazon, are capturing strong consumer interest. The convergence of information technology and telecommunications will lead to a whole new wave of innovations in communications and the digital management of content of all kinds.

The healthcare sector has also witnessed high levels of innovation with the development of new drugs, medical devices and health management software, underpinned by world-class scientific research. Nevertheless, major pharmaceutical companies are faced with significant innovation challenges, as many of their blockbuster drugs come off patent and new drug pipelines have become relatively lean. However, designer drugs are now within the realms of possibility due to recent rapid advances in human genomics. The possibility of anti-aging drugs could become a reality if new research based on sirtuin protein super-stimulators proves to be successful. Stem cell research also holds promise for a more radical approach to aging that involves growing spare tissues and organs that could be replaced as required. Robotics are now inside the operating theatre and some 50% of prostate surgical procedures in the US are now being carried out remotely by a surgeon using computer-controlled arms.

Clean and renewable energy is high on the agendas of governments around the globe and the development of innovative technologies to reduce the dependence on fossil fuels has gained significant momentum. Plug-in electric cars are on the verge of becoming a reality as new generation lithium-ion batteries offer a major step forward in performance. A number of countries, such as the EU and the US, are introducing new legislation to phase out the energy-hungry, incandescent light bulb by 2012.

The renewable energy sector is flourishing with some 30-40 gigawatts of renewable power installed around the world and new innovative technologies in the pipeline; this is being strongly supported by venture capital of some $20 billion currently invested globally in start-up companies in 2007. Thin-film solar technology is attracting strong interest with companies such as Nanosolar in the US deploying nanotechnology to develop a new thin layer panel system that promises to significantly reduce the cost of generating solar electricity.

The next generation of biofuels, which can process cellulosic biomass, and therefore do not compete with food crops, are already well advanced into the pilot plant phase. Even the software giant, Google has announced a new strategic initiative to develop electricity from renewable energy resources. Their goal is to produce one gigawatt (enough to power a city the size of San Francisco) of renewable energy capacity that is cheaper than coal, within years rather than decades, and with an initial focus on advanced solar and wind power technologies.

The term nanotechnology has become the modern terminology to describe miniaturization that approaches the level of 1–100 nm (a nanometre is 1/billionth of a metre). A Californian start-up company called A123 has developed a new generation of lithium-ion batteries based on the discovery of a new nano-phosphate material by researchers at the Massachusetts Institute of Technology (MIT). This new nano-material exhibits electrical properties that enable lithium-ion batteries to be produced with double the power density and much faster recharging than conventional systems, and therefore promises a quantum step forward in battery technology.

The emergence of new innovative multinational companies such as Haier, Lenovo, Huawei and CMC from China, and the Tata Group, Ranbaxy Laboratories and Suzlon from India demonstrate the growing prowess of these large, rapidly emerging countries. The recent launch by the Tata Group of the Nano car, priced at $2,500, provides an example of the disruptive low-cost innovation model that will increasingly challenge high-cost developed countries in the future. Venture capital that has historically been a major driving force for innovation in the US continues to grow rapidly and is spreading globally into rapidly developing countries such as China and India. Multinational companies are investing in new research and development facilities to promote innovation for new products and services in these large and fast growing Asian economies and thereby participate in the low-cost innovation model.

The cycles of economic growth that are coupled to waves of innovation, first identified by Schumpeter, are becoming shorter, which is indicative of a structural trend of innovation acceleration. This increased speed of innovation is underpinned by the almost explosive rate of growth in knowledge emerging from global research in science and technology. The development of vibrant innovation infrastructures at both the company and country level will be vital to achieve sustainable financial performance and GDP growth, respectively.

Innovation will undoubtedly not only drive economic growth but will also play a major role in tackling some of the most challenging issues that face the world in the next few decades such as climate change, environmental pollution, fossil fuel shortages, third world poverty, rising healthcare costs and aging populations.

Acknowledgments

The author is very grateful to many people who have provided inspiration and support to make this book possible.

Special thanks are due to Dr. Roger Downing, who has tirelessly provided high-quality editing and invaluable critique throughout the writing of the manuscript.

The author is also grateful to William Harbidge and Caz Hopkins for their excellent design and graphical skills that have produced the figures in the book.

I am also in debt to the many colleagues from Shell International in Europe and the US with whom I have had the pleasure of working together on many innovative and successful projects.

I could not have enjoyed the remarkable and challenging experience of co-founding and managing two start-up companies, Avantium and Crystallics, without the financial support of the Shell Group and founding investors. Moreover, without the enthusiasm and dedication of the founding management and technical teams of these companies, the sustained growth and success would not have been achieved.

Following the author's return to New Zealand, the period with Auckland Uniservices provided valuable insight into innovation within an academic environment.

The author is also grateful to the software team and management at NetValue, and Ross Vernall for their support in launching R&D Tools, to develop online software to enable organizations to more effectively manage their R&D and innovation.

Most importantly, the author would like to thank his family for their patience and support during the many days, evenings and weekends that he has devoted to researching and writing this book.

About the Author

The career of the author, Ian E. Maxwell, has encompassed science, technology and innovation in Shell International, in Europe and the US at the senior executive level, the founding and CEO positions in three high technology start-up companies and a general manager position in a university technology commercialization organization.

He is currently the CEO of both the Maxco Consulting Group and R&D Tools (www.rdtools.co.nz), a company with a focus on developing and globally marketing web-based software tools to enhance R&D management and innovation. The *R&D Portfolio Management*^{TM} software product, for example, is well suited to enable companies and research organizations to readily and very cost effectively implement R&D portfolio management systems resulting in significantly improved innovation productivity.

The author has a PhD in Chemistry and is the co-author of some 80 scientific, technology review articles and book chapters. He is also the co-inventor of some 25 patents that have been filed internationally and has been an invited speaker at many international science, technology and innovation conferences.

Contents

Chapter 1
Innovation and Economic Growth

It is now widely recognized that innovation is a key growth driver and, therefore, a high priority for senior executives worldwide. The top ranking companies around the world in terms of sustainable growth and profitability are leaders in innovation. Most companies, however, have not yet developed a robust infrastructure encompassing the processes and tools needed to successfully innovate and are, therefore, seriously at risk in the new global innovation race. Building a strong innovation infrastructure is considerably more complex than, for example, implementing a quality programme such as Six Sigma. Companies that embrace innovation and build well-managed systems to ensure that innovation permeates the entire company culture will very likely achieve sustainable high revenue growth and strong shareholder returns.

Countries are also increasingly recognizing the importance of innovation as a driver for Gross Domestic Product (GDP) growth and many are proactively taking measures to create the right infrastructure to facilitate innovation.

Furthermore, countries that build both a foundation of science and technology and a strong innovation infrastructure will experience strong GDP growth and high living standards, as measured by GDP per capita. By contrast, countries that are unable to create and sustain an innovation foundation and infrastructure, will struggle to compete and raise living standards in the increasingly competitive global economy.

1.1 Innovation Waves

Innovation is not new; the Russian economist, Nikolai Kondratiev (1892–1938), was the first to identify major long-wave economic cycles associated with capitalist economies. The innovation theory ascribed these waves to the bunching of basic innovations that launch technological revolutions that, in turn, create new leading industrial or business sectors. Kondratiev's early ideas were taken up by the economist, Joseph Schumpeter (1883–1950), in the 1930s, who developed a theory which predicted the existence of very long-run macroeconomic cycles, originally estimated to last 50–55 years.

I.E. Maxwell, *Managing Sustainable Innovation*,
DOI 10.1007/978-0-387-87581-1_1, © 2009 by Ian E. Maxwell

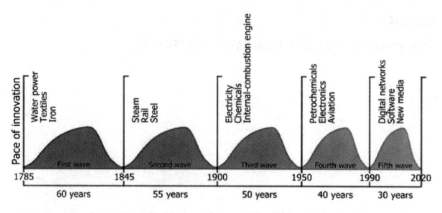

Fig. 1.1 The Schumpeter innovation waves (Author's drawing)

Schumpeter is, perhaps, best known for his work showing the link between entrepreneurial discovery and economic progress in the form of five waves of industrial innovation. Crucially, these waves show a decreasing frequency which indicates that innovation is accelerating. The current pace of innovation is such that there appears to be every reason to believe that the Schumpeter theory is correct and that we are currently moving out of the fifth wave and therefore rapidly approaching the next innovation wave as shown in Fig. 1.1.

Schumpeter also believed that innovation is the driving force not only of capitalism, but also of economic progress in general, and that entrepreneurs are the agents of innovation. Interestingly, he also feared that "entrepreneurial capitalism would not flourish because the bureaucracies of modern government and big corporations would dampen innovation". Moreover, he was also concerned that "the importance of entrepreneurs would fade over time as capitalism sought predictability from governments who would plan economic activity as well as order social benefits". Schumpeter showed great foresight in this regard as we now observe the race for governments to remove the barriers of bureaucracy and create a strong infrastructure in which innovation will flourish.

1.2 Country Innovation Ranking

Recently, there have been some interesting attempts to quantify and rank countries with regard to innovation on the basis of a number of input and output parameters.

INSEAD, the top-tier, Paris-based business school, has recently taken up this, not insignificant, challenge of attempting to measure country levels of innovation. The so-called Global Innovation Index (GII) is intended to give a clearer picture of a country's strengths and deficiencies with respect to innovation-related policies and practices.

The GII model relies upon eight pillars made up of five inputs and three outputs that they believe underpin the factors that enhance innovative capacity and demonstrate results from successful innovation. The model uses a combination of objective and subjective data drawn from a variety of public and private sources. Objective data comes from sources such as the World Bank, International Telecommunications Union (e.g. university enrolment rates, GDP growth rates, the level of penetration of new technologies) and subjective data is drawn from the World Economic Forum's annual Executive Opinion Survey.

Examples of the subjective data include concepts such as the quality of corporate governance, the overall excellence of scientific institutions and the quality of intellectual property rights protections. The framework groups the eight pillars of innovation into two Input and Output categories. Input pillars represent aspects which enhance the capacity of a nation to generate ideas and leverage them for innovative products and services.

The five Input pillars:

- Institutions and Policies.
- Human Capacity.
- Infrastructure.
- Technological Sophistication.
- Business Markets and Capital.

Output pillars represent the ultimate benefits of innovation for a nation such as, more knowledge creation, increased competitiveness and greater wealth generation. The three Output pillars:

- Knowledge.
- Competitiveness.
- Wealth.

Each pillar of the GII model is measured by a number of quantitative and qualitative variables. The averaged scores for the Input and Output pillars together give an overall score – the Global Innovation Index. More detailed information on the calculation of the GII is given on the INSEAD web site.

The country GII rankings and scores for 2007 are as follows:

1. US 5.80
2. Germany 4.89
3. UK 4.81
4. Japan 4.48
5. France 4.32
6. Switzerland 4.16
7. Singapore 4.10
8. Canada 4.06

  9. Netherlands 3.99
10. Hong Kong   3.97

In parallel, the Organization for Economic Cooperation and Development (OECD) has also developed a so-called Global Innovation Scoreboard (GIS) for countries in which they measure the following parameters:

- Innovation drivers.
- Knowledge creation.
- Diffusion.
- Applications.
- Intellectual property.

These parameters are then combined to calculate a Global Summary Innovation Index (GSII). Interestingly, when the GDP per capita for each country is plotted against the GSII, there is a positive correlation. This indicates that countries that have a strong innovation infrastructure that is efficiently utilised, will enjoy a high level of wealth creation as shown in Fig. 1.2.

Fig. 1.2 GDP per capita and Global Summary Innovation Index, GSII (Source: OECD Country Innovation Reports)

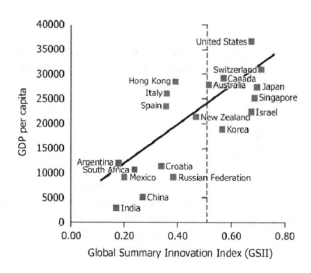

These innovation parameters can also be seen as a combination of building a science and technology foundation to support an innovation infrastructure from which new or improved products, processes and services are created as shown in Fig. 1.3.

Top ranking innovation countries such as the US have both a strong foundation and a robust innovation infrastructure. Lower ranking countries such as China have spent the past few decades building a strong science and technology foundation and are now at an early phase of building an innovation infrastructure. This solid

Fig. 1.3 Country innovation building blocks (Author's drawing)

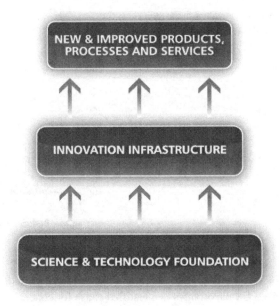

foundation and announced ambition to accelerate the development of the innovation infrastructure means that their ranking will likely climb rapidly in the near future. Countries like India that have not yet built such a strong science and technology foundation but are developing the innovation infrastructure are also expected to climb in ranking but, perhaps, not at the same rate as China.

Russia has a highly educated workforce but needs to modernize science and technology foundation and build an innovation infrastructure. If the petrodollars were invested wisely, Russia has the potential to build a more balanced economy. Some of the oil-rich countries in the Middle East, such as the United Arab Emirates (UAE), are already demonstrating a longer term vision, and are using their enormous cash reserves to build both the foundation and the infrastructure to achieve a more sustainable, innovation-driven economy in the future.

1.3 US Innovation Dominance

The US continues to dominate the country innovation rankings, achieving a top ranking for both the GII and GSII scoring systems. However, there has recently been quite some debate as to whether the US is in danger of losing this top innovation position. The increased importance of innovation to productivity growth in the US is clearly demonstrated in Fig. 1.4.

The concern in the US has been largely focused around a perceived erosion of the science and technology foundation that supports the innovation infrastructure.

Fig. 1.4 Growth of innovation and productivity in the US (redrawn from source)

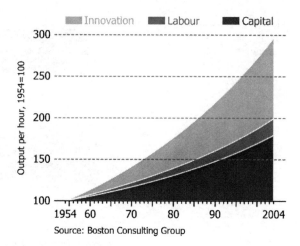

Source: Boston Consulting Group

Indeed, the decreasing number of science and technology graduates being produced from US universities is a justified cause for concern.

In addition, perhaps, one of the greatest challenges to the US and other developed countries is the low-cost innovation model emerging from China and India. Furthermore, the endemically weak US energy policy and growing dependence on increasingly high-cost, imported oil has made the country very vulnerable to disruptions in this crucial market. Hence, the US economy and technology base is ill prepared for the new era of highly priced fossil fuels. The current crisis facing the US automobile industry, which has been based around fuel-inefficient cars, and the serious threat now posed from Japanese hybrid and plug-in technology vehicles, is an example of the vulnerability of some major sectors of the US economy.

In contrast, the speed with which Silicon Valley venture capital has responded to this crisis with a surge of investment into start-up companies developing clean and renewable energy technologies is a reflection of the remarkable financial resources and adaptability of the innovation infrastructure in the US. It remains to be seen, however, whether Silicon Valley can indeed successfully challenge the traditional energy companies and create a new generation of clean and renewable energy giants and, thereby, compensate for the crisis facing the vulnerable energy intensive sectors of the US economy.

1.4 Company Innovation Rankings

Companies around the globe are starting to critically review their innovation capabilities. Procter & Gamble (P&G), the world's biggest consumer-products firm, studied the life cycle of consumer goods in America from 1992 to 2002 and concluded that they now need to innovate twice as fast. The 3M company, famous for inventing the Post-it sticky note, also believes the world is moving much faster and that they need to be talking to customers much earlier in the innovation process to try to shorten development times. Siemens, the German multinational, is adamant that innovation is happening much faster and predicts an explosion of medical know-how due to the advance of information technology into medicine.

In recent years, the magazine, Business Week, in collaboration with the Boston Consulting Group (BCG), has produced an annual innovation ranking of global companies and the results are shown for 2008 in Fig. 1.5.

The methodology used gives the following weightings to achieve the final ranking: votes cast by a survey of about 3,000 company executives 80%; last three year revenue and margin growth 5%; last three year stock returns 5%. While it may be argued that this methodology is not perfect, it does provide an attempt to quantify company innovation and relate this to financial performance.

In 2008, based on this ranking system, Apple is the clear leader with strong average growth rates in all categories, followed by Google who were significantly weaker in margin growth. Both these companies are identified with remarkable innovation infrastructures that create, develop and market successful, new global

COMPANY INNOVATION RANKINGS 2008 (BUSINESS WEEK & BCG)

Rank	Company	HQ Country	Revenue Growth 2004-07 (in %)	Margin Growth 2004-07 (in %)	Stock Returns 2004-07 (in %)
1	APPLE	USA	47	69	83
2	GOOGLE	USA	73	5	53
3	TOYOTA MOTOR	Japan	12	1	15
4	GENERAL ELECTRIC	USA	9	1	3
5	MICROSOFT	USA	16	8	12
6	TATA GROUP	India	na	na	na
7	NINTENDO	Japan	37	4	77
8	PROCTER & GAMBLE	USA	16	4	12
9	SONY	Japan	8	13	17
10	NOKIA	Finland	20	2	35
11	AMAZON.COM	USA	29	−11	28
12	IBM	USA	1	11	4
13	RESEARCH IN MOTION	Canada	56	−1	51
14	BMW	Germany	6	−5	11
15	HEWLETT-PACKARD	USA	10	17	35
16	HONDA MOTOR	Japan	12	6	14
17	WALT DISNEY	USA	6	14	7
18	GENERAL MOTORS	USA	−2	na	−11
19	RELIANCE INDUSTRIES	India	31	−7	94
20	BOEING	USA	9	32	21

Fig. 1.5 Company innovation rankings 2008
(Source: Business Week; redrawn from source)

products at breakneck speed. Toyota also ranks well, largely due to their foresight to launch the innovative hybrid electric car well ahead of competitors. It is also noteworthy, that almost 50% of the top 20 ranked companies are from outside the US which reflects a trend towards wide spread and global growth of innovation.

Chapter 2
Innovation Concepts

Some concepts are introduced which are intended to provide insight into the various types and modes of innovation. Many of these innovation concepts will be referred to in other parts of the book.

2.1 Innovation Types

Innovation is often linked to new technology but this perception is too simplistic as it may take a number of forms or innovation types. The most common innovation types include: product, process, service and business models as shown in Fig. 2.1.

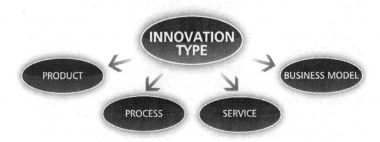

Fig. 2.1 Types of innovation (Author's drawing)

A new hand-held music player, such as the iPod, or a new mobile phone such as the iPhone are recent examples of product innovation. Other examples involving major research and development investments include the Prius electric-gasoline hybrid car from Toyota and the A380 super jumbo aircraft from Airbus.

The development of new manufacturing routes to produce automotive fuels from renewable plant sources, such as sugar cane or corn (termed first generation biofuels), instead of conventional crude oil refining, is an example of process innovation. The production of ethanol from sugar cane, for use as a gasoline additive, has become widely practised in Brazil for many years and biofuels from other plant sources are

I.E. Maxwell, *Managing Sustainable Innovation*,
DOI 10.1007/978-0-387-87581-1_2, © 2009 by Ian E. Maxwell

now rapidly developing in other parts of the world. Gas-to-liquids (GTL) technology has been developed by Shell, Exxon, Sasol and others to convert remote natural gas to a "clean" liquid hydrocarbon product that can be used as a high quality diesel fuel and as a feedstock for the manufacture of detergents and lubeoil. These new processes make use of advanced processes deploying sophisticated catalyst systems that greatly enhance the efficiency and, therefore, the economics of these process innovations. A number of large scale GTL plants are currently under construction in Qatar where natural gas is plentiful but the large consumer markets are remote.

At the other end of the manufacturing scale, in the field of micro-electronics, transistor density has increased rapidly enabling the production of ever smaller and more powerful devices such as flash memory chips (used in the nano iPod), integrated circuits (used in laptops) and hard disc drives (used in large digital storage devices). The umbrella term, nanotechnology, which embraces the application of innovative technology at the near atomic scale, is currently a "hot" topic with venture capital companies and promises to create a new wave of product innovation.

Downloading music from an iPod and payment through the internet using the Apple iTunes software are examples of service innovation. The Google offering of a free, powerful internet search engine and generating revenues by targeted advertising "clicks" is an example of business model innovation.

The above examples relate to different types of innovations that have been successfully brought to the market. In some cases, the market entry may involve a combination of innovation types. For example, Google developed a highly advanced internet search engine which could be considered as a service innovation but chose an innovative business model to generate dramatic growth in revenues, profitability and shareholder value from this technology. In fact, this Google business innovation has created a whole new business model paradigm within the IT industry. The biofuel example given above could also be viewed as a combination of a process and product innovation.

Interestingly, Gary Hamel, the founder of the consulting company, Strategos, is of the view that business model innovators have reaped the greatest rewards in recent decades. This observation is probably counter-intuitive to what most people would have believed. This would suggest that companies and organizations that are focused on product, process and service innovation should also reflect on their business models for potential high added value overall outcomes.

An example of business model innovation which has had a major impact in poor countries such as Bangladesh, is the Grameen Bank. This is a microfinance organization and community development bank started in Bangladesh that makes small loans, called microcredits, to the impoverished without requiring collateral. The system is based on the idea that the poor have skills that are under utilized. The bank also accepts deposits, provides other services, and runs several development-oriented businesses including fabric, telephone and energy companies. The organization and its founder, Muhammad Yunus, were jointly awarded the Nobel Peace Prize in 2006. The Bank today continues to expand across the nation and still provides small loans to the rural poor. As of mid-2006, the Grameen Bank branches numbered over 2,100 and its success has inspired similar projects around the world.

2.2 Innovation Modes

Innovation can occur across a wide range of economic, scientific, technological, educational, sociological and artistic human activities. This book will primarily focus on economic, scientific and technological innovation.

Innovation can also have quite differing degrees of transformation which can be divided into three classes which are termed incremental, quantum and disruptive as shown in Fig. 2.2.

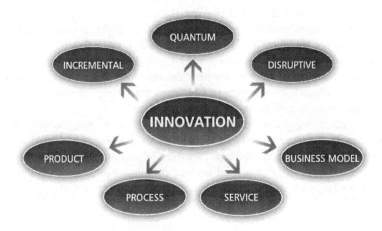

Fig. 2.2 Modes and types of innovation (Author's drawing)

2.3 Incremental Innovation

Incremental innovation relates to modest stepwise improvements in a technology as is illustrated in a so-called "S-curve" shown in Fig. 2.3.

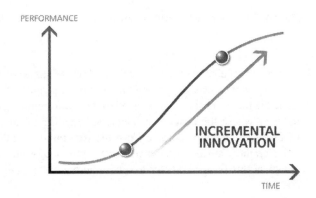

Fig. 2.3 S-curve for incremental innovation (Author's drawing)

An example of incremental innovation would be the evolution of the modern motor vehicle whereby the features of performance, reliability, safety, fuel economy, comfort and relative cost have been gradually improved over many years. Another example would be the integrated circuit where miniaturization and computing power have also improved dramatically over the past 10 years and has, in fact, closely followed Moore's law. In 1965, Moore examined the density of transistors at which cost is minimized, and observed that, as transistors were made smaller through advances in photolithography, the number of these components would increase at "a rate of roughly a factor of two every two years".

Interestingly, computer hard drive and flash memory technologies have also experienced steep incremental performance gains at reduced costs. These steep experience curves have provided ever more advanced computers and have enabled the development of increasingly powerful and complex software systems.

Companies competing in this incremental technology space must maintain their levels of research and development to keep pace with these performance improvement relationships or their products become obsolete.

The so-called "experience curve" is an example of incremental innovation in which a continuous research and development effort is deployed to drive down product costs with time, normally through improvements in manufacturing. The rate of cost decrease is normally exponential with the cumulative number of units produced resulting in a linear logarithmic relationship as shown in Fig. 2.4.

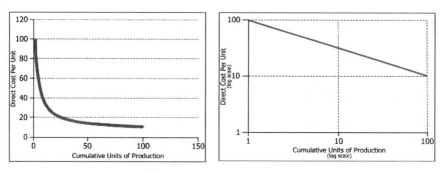

Fig. 2.4 Exponential and logarithmic experience curves (Author's drawing)

The rate of cost reduction as measured by the slopes of these "experience curves" can vary enormously depending on the type of product; for example, in bulk chemicals, the rate of cost reduction is relatively slow compared to the modern electronic industry where the costs of products such as digital memory devices, flat screen LCD TV and lap top computers decline very rapidly. In the fast moving electronics industry, these steep "experience curves" pose major innovation challenges to companies in this business sector to remain at the cutting edge of both technology and costs.

2.4 Quantum Innovation

Quantum innovation involves a major improvement to an existing technology that displaces current technology as illustrated in an "S-curve" shown in Fig. 2.5.

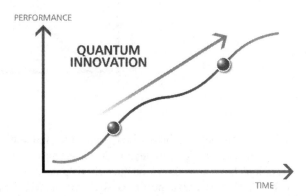

Fig. 2.5 S-curve for quantum innovation (Author's drawing)

Recent examples include the iPod and the nano-iPod from Apple that displaced the once ubiquitous Sony Walkman mobile music player. The Da Vinci robotic surgery from Intuitive Surgery is rapidly displacing conventional open and even laparoscopic surgery. Open source computer software such as Linux, now widely applied by companies such as IBM, is steadily replacing proprietary systems such as those from Microsoft. It remains to be seen if the Apple i-phone and the Google Android open source mobile phone software will become quantum innovations and displace existing mobile telephone hardware and software, respectively.

2.5 Disruptive Innovation

Disruptive innovation involves the development of a new product or process that is such a marked improvement that it eventually makes the current technology completely redundant as shown in Fig. 2.6.

One example of disruptive innovation was the replacement of film photography with digital cameras and images. Kodak, the past leader in the photographic business, was slow to recognize that digital technology would eventually displace film and has since struggled to survive. Interestingly, the shift to digital also attracted new players such as Sony from the electronics industry who brought competencies that were valuable to innovate in the new era of digital images.

In communications, the Internet has almost completely displaced the mechanical transfer of documents and has had a huge impact on the speed and efficiency of document management in the modern office although the paperless office has not yet emerged.

Fig. 2.6 S-curve for
disruptive innovation
(Author's drawing)

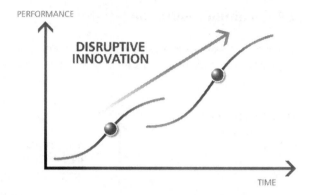

Mobile phones are increasingly replacing fixed line communications and in some countries are now already the dominant means of communication. Flat screen televisions have now almost completely displaced the older TV tubes while liquid crystal displays (LCD) appear to be winning out over the more energy-intensive and shorter lifetime plasma technology. In the medical area, non-invasive, 3-dimensional medical technologies such as computer tomography (CT), magnetic resonance imaging (MRI) and ultrasound have now displaced many previously inaccurate or invasive diagnostic techniques. Although very much in their infancy, personalized drugs could potentially displace the "one fits all" blockbuster medicines that are currently the core business of the major pharmaceutical companies.

The Google business model, to offer free search services and monetize through internet advertising, has been disruptive to other software business models. Customers are becoming used to having access to advanced search technology and even free software which is funded through advertising revenue.

Open source software is also becoming more disruptive as the reliability and performance improves to the extent that it is displacing proprietary, license fee-based software. For example, the open source operating system, Linux, is now being adopted and even supported by multinational companies such as IBM. Major universities around the world are starting to embrace open source software to offer web based e-learning platforms to their students, teachers and administrators.

Social network software such as YouTube and Face Book is rapidly replacing the telephone as a communication medium for the younger generation.

2.6 Innovation Cycles and Sustainability

The various modes of innovation are characterized by a different economic benefit and risk profile as shown in Fig. 2.7.

Disruptive innovation, while having the highest potential economic benefit, also has the highest risk in terms of success. Incremental innovation is at the other end of the spectrum with quantum innovation in between. In order to maintain growth

Fig. 2.7 Economic
benefit/risk profiles for
innovation modes (Author's
drawing)

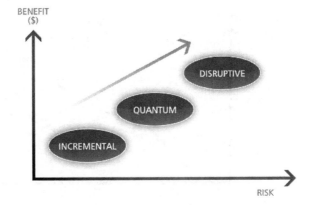

and balance risk, it is very important for companies to analyse their research and development portfolios in terms of the spread of projects across these innovation modes.

Successful high-growth companies appear to have achieved the right balance between quantum and incremental innovation projects. A quantum innovation is followed by incremental innovation to improve the product, process or service, while the next quantum innovation is under development. The frequency of quantum and incremental innovation will vary widely depending on the specific business sector. For example, in software development, the time to market will, in general, be relatively short for both modes of innovation. By contrast, in the pharmaceutical sector, the quantum innovation time will often be as long as a decade due to the extended toxicity and clinical trial testing that are required by the government authorities before a new drug can be safely launched in the market. Similarly, for the energy and bulk chemicals sector, given the complexity of process scale-up, the time required to develop and launch a new quantum innovation can also be on a decade scale.

A top ranking innovation company, such as Apple, has the capability to efficiently manage the cycle of quantum and incremental mode. New quantum innovative products such as the iPod, are launched and rapidly capture a significant global market share. A series of incremental innovations follow, such as the nano-iPod, to maintain market share. To sustain high growth, the next quantum innovation such as the iPhone is launched and incremental improvements, such as 3G capability, and a range of new applications rapidly follow as shown in Fig. 2.8.

To achieve this remarkable performance, Apple likely has separate teams managing the quantum and incremental developments to ensure that they maintain a balanced research and development portfolio. Another quantum innovation from Apple would appear to be planned with the possible launch of a laptop using only flash memory and displacing the current hard drive technology.

Other companies in the same business sector, such as Sony, seem to struggle with this balance. For example, the Sony Walkman was a quantum innovation but the further development appears to have become locked into small incremental improvements, providing an opening for a quantum innovation which Apple captured with

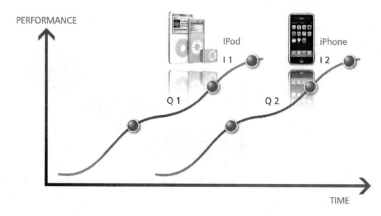

Fig. 2.8 Quantum and incremental innovation cycles (Author's drawing)

the iPod. Although by no means certain, the strong customer response to the innovative Kindle e-book from Amazon suggests that the Sony e-book may also be displaced by a quantum innovation from an online sales company.

Many other large Asian companies in the electronics business sector also seem to be locked into incremental innovation and, together with their competitors, are struggling to maintain both revenue growth and acceptable product margins. Increased quantum innovation will likely be the only way forward for these companies to achieve sustainable high growth rates.

Google is another good example of a successful high growth company that proactively manages quantum and incremental innovation. The Google research and development culture is strongly aligned towards quantum innovation and they continue to both surprise and delight the market with novel new products beyond Google search. These include Google Earth, Google desktop search, Google image search, Google AdSense, Google Analytics, Google Small Business Apps, Google 101 Cloud, Google Renewable Energy cheaper than Coal, and Google Android mobile software and, undoubtedly, there are many more Google innovations in the pipeline. Perhaps, more than any other company, Google could be faced with the luxury of an imbalance towards quantum innovation, which may mean that their resources for incremental innovation to maintain market share for their existing products are heavily stretched. The increasing diversity of their business model will also likely present some challenges to Google in the future but their high level of quantum innovation is to be admired.

Many multinational oil and gas companies appear to be locked into long-term incremental innovation projects which largely target modest improvements in fossil fuel related technology. By contrast, small start-up companies supported by global venture capital are announcing quantum innovation steps in the burgeoning high growth renewable energy sector. Big oil is also strongly challenged to discover replacements for their oil and gas reserves as national oil companies become more protective of the increasingly scarce resources. This suggests that the business models of multinational oil companies will need to embrace a larger proportion of quantum innovation if they are to sustain growth in the new global energy landscape. The recent announcements by Shell, for example, of partnerships with smaller innovative renewable energy companies would seem to indicate a strategic shift in the right direction.

In the healthcare sector, relatively new, large biotech companies such as Amgen and Genentech have a strong focus on sustained quantum innovation with strong pipelines of innovative drugs. Incremental innovation will generally involve improved formulations and manufacturing technology for a particular proprietary drug. In contrast, many large traditional pharmaceutical companies are more focused on incremental innovation around existing drugs rather than the higher risk quantum innovation associated with a new type of drug. A shift in strategy will likely be required to achieve a better quantum and incremental innovation balance and restore high revenue growth. The acquisition of small innovative biotech companies is a strategy that big pharma often deploys to achieve quantum innovation.

Disruptive innovation is very difficult to plan and will likely emerge unexpectedly from research projects that are focused on quantum innovation. Thus, companies such as Google and Apple, with a strong quantum innovation culture, will be expected to achieve the occasional disruptive innovation.

Chapter 3
Innovation Infrastructure

Considering the crucial importance of innovation, it is surprising that the development and management of an innovation infrastructure is still embryonic compared with other aspects of business management. However, the development of an efficient innovation infrastructure has now become a top priority with companies that strive to become high-growth global leaders.

3.1 Innovation Tipping Points

The term innovation is normally used to describe the complete process from idea creation through delivery of the new product, process or service into the market. This will usually involve a number of steps such as, idea or invention, an induction phase, a development phase and the launch in the market. The inflection point at which the innovation moves out of the induction phase and enjoys rapid growth in the market is termed the "innovation tipping point" as shown in Fig. 3.1.

Fig. 3.1 Innovation "tipping point" (Author's drawing)

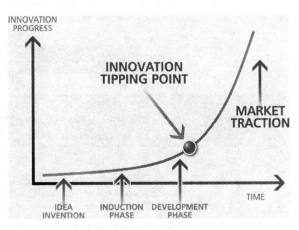

The time to reach this "tipping point" can vary enormously whereby the induction phase could, for example, be quite long spanning a number of years. There are many examples of technologies that have been invented many years before the market conditions were right for adoption. The now ubiquitous computer mouse is an example of a technology that went through a long induction phase. The development phase can also be quite long in certain business sectors such as drug development, where the toxicity testing and clinical trials can take up to 10 years, with current costs of between $500 million and $1 billion per drug. Likewise, for new large-scale industrial processes in the chemicals, power generation and fuel processing industries, the development time can often span up to a decade.

In contrast, modern software development can be very rapid, with new upgrades being designed, developed and launched in the market within months. The new "software for service" IT business model enables upgrades and new products to be seamlessly and rapidly launched from the developers' servers directly to the customers. Examples of technologies that have had long induction phases followed by rapid market traction after passing through a tipping point include the internet, wind energy, solar energy, gas to liquids (GTL) fuels, open source software, laptop computers, LED lighting, robotic surgery, hybrid cars, cloud computing and electronic touch screens.

3.2 Innovation Value Chain

The innovation value chain encompasses the various phases of development of a new product, process or service which includes research development, manufacturing and marketing as shown in Fig. 3.2.

However, this is not a linear process and, for example, early feedback from the market can be vital to ensure that the research, development and manufacturing steps are tuned to the customer's needs and adjusted as market conditions change.

Fig. 3.2 Innovation value chain management (Author's drawing)

The efficient management of this value chain has become crucial to minimizing costs and achieving "speed to market". Globalization has also had a major impact on the management of this value chain as companies now need to objectively decide in which location or country they can best execute each of these components.

While the outsourcing of manufacturing to low labour cost countries such as China, India and more recently Vietnam, has been a strong trend for the last decade, other parts of the value chain are now also moving offshore. Research and development, for example, is now also shifting to China and India where there is a rapidly growing resource of low cost and highly educated labour. Companies such as Microsoft, Google, Intel, Sun Microsystems, Adobe Systems, P&G, Toyota and Schlumberger have, in recent years, set up research and development facilities in China. Similarly, multinationals such as Shell, General Electric (GE), Unilever and Google now have research laboratories in India.

Clearly, this trend towards the globalization of the innovation value chain also creates new management challenges involving the coordination of complex projects where the various components are executed in different countries.

3.3 Innovation Phases

The management of innovation may be considered as a two-part selection project process in which the best innovations pass through the funnel into the market as shown in Fig. 3.3.

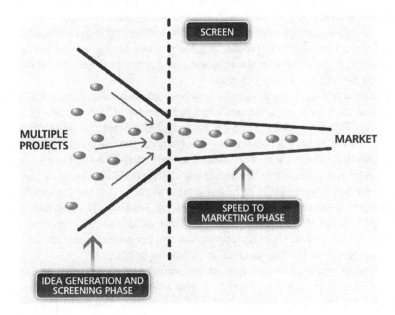

Fig. 3.3 Innovation management phases (Author's drawing)

The first, so-called "Idea Generation and Screening Phase", involves the screening of a large number of ideas that have been generated from a wide variety of sources, both internal and external. Many of these ideas may have been generated through an "open Innovation" process which will be discussed in more detail later.

The second phase, the so-called "Speed to Market Phase", involves the management of a portfolio of projects that have passed through the "Idea Generation and Screening Phase" as shown in the figure above. Although the quality of the Idea Generation phase is very important, the management of the follow-on innovation process is equally important due to the risks and costs involved as well as managing the time to market. It is often this "Speed to Market Phase" that is often poorly managed, which results in either failure or long and costly delays in the launch of the new product or service.

3.4 Portfolio Management

Most companies and research organizations have R&D portfolios that consist of large numbers of projects covering the whole range from early stage screening of ideas through to market launch. In many companies, these projects tend to be managed in a rather ad hoc manner with a small group of senior managers deciding on the funding and resources that are allocated to each project.

A more structured and proactive management of these project portfolios, which is the core of the corporate innovation engine, can dramatically increase the innovation output of the company and, thereby, boost revenue growth.

A well-defined screening process is essential for the first phase of innovation and a gated project management process is good practice for the second phase. While the concepts of project portfolio management and gating have been around for some time, they are still not widely practised.

Innovative software tools, such as new web-based products from *R&D Tools,* can enable these quite complex processes to be managed both efficiently and cost effectively. This online software tool is based on the concept that projects should be managed on the basis of a balance between business attractiveness, risk and cumulative cost. Projects are carefully evaluated using a scoring process to quantify each project in terms of these three key components. The portfolio of projects can then be easily reviewed using a matrix of business attractiveness, risk and cumulative costs.

On the basis of a well-defined scoring process, attractive projects will be in the "top right" sectors of the matrix where "business attractiveness" is medium or high and "risk" is medium to high. The cumulative cost per project is introduced into this matrix as the size of the "project bubble" as shown in Fig. 3.4.

The matrix provides an overview of the portfolio of projects and enables management to track progress proactively. It also forms the basis for decisions on the continued funding of the projects in the R&D portfolio. The evaluation technique

Fig. 3.4 Project portfolio management (Author's drawing)

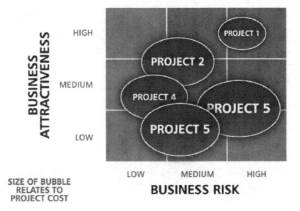

involves scoring a series of questions related to business attractiveness and risk. Weighting factors related to each of these questions can also be included as well as a "no-go" option if specific questions score below a certain threshold level. The questions can be customized to any organization but should then be "normalized" to ensure that the relative scores remain valid for the innovation process for the whole portfolio of projects (Figs. 3.5 and 3.6).

	CRITERIA	Score (1-5)	Weighting (%)	Total score
1	Fit with company growth strategy	5	100	5.00
2	Fit with company skills and resources	5	75	3.75
3	Revenue growth potential	5	75	3.75
4	Competitive advantage	5	100	5.00
5	Global growth opportunities	5	75	3.75
6	R&D costs	5	75	3.75
7	Business model scalability	5	75	3.75
		Grand total		28.75

High	35-28	100-80%
Medium	27-21	77-60%
Low	20-0	57-0%

Fig. 3.5 Project business attractiveness analysis (Author's drawing)

CRITERIA	Score (1-5)	Weighting (%)	Total score
1 Technical risk	5	100	5.00
2 Speed to market risk	5	100	5.00
3 IP/Copyright protection risk	5	100	5.00
4 Global competition risk	5	100	5.00
5 Market development risk	5	100	5.00
6 Geographical political risk	5	75	3.75
Grand total			28.75

High risk	30-24	100-80%
Medium risk	23-18	77-60%
Low risk	17-0	57-0%

Fig. 3.6 Project risk analysis (Author's drawing)

Clearly, the project evaluations are only as good as the quality of the input data. It is therefore recommended that teams with diverse skills are used to carry out the project scoring to increase objectivity and provide balanced input.

3.5 Project Gating Process

This project portfolio management can be further enhanced by the use of a gating process whereby projects are evaluated at regular intervals along the innovation pathway. For example, during technology development, business development and during market launch as shown in Fig. 3.7 four gates have been included.

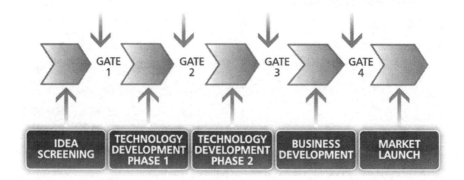

Fig. 3.7 Project gating process (Author's drawing)

Projects are re-evaluated at each gate and placed in the business attractive-ness/risk/cost matrix. The locus of projects within this matrix at each gate can then be tracked and used as a portfolio management decision-making tool. As a project moves down the innovation pathway, the quality of the evaluation input data will normally improve as the depth and breadth of knowledge related to technology and business development increases.

For example, if a project moves in the direction of lower business attractiveness and high risk, a decision might be made to terminate this project. This so-called "fast failure" is essential to ensure that limited company resources are being deployed on projects with the highest chance of achieving commercial success. In contrast, if a project moves in the opposite direction whereby business attractiveness improves and risk does not increase, a decision might be made to enhance speed to market by increasing spending on this project as is illustrated in Fig. 3.8.

Fig. 3.8 Project gating profile (Author's drawing)

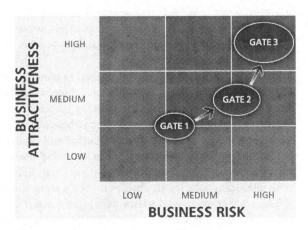

The distribution of projects between gates can also be monitored to ensure that there is the right balance of projects moving forward. In addition, the tool can also be used for scenario planning whereby projects can be evaluated for business attrac-tiveness/risk/cost based on assumptions looking forward into the future. A portfolio of projects based on these forward projections can then be developed and analysed in terms of the profiles. Moreover, a number of portfolio scenarios can be developed in this manner with different risk profiles, for strategic planning purposes at the executive senior management and/or Board level. The *R&D Tools* software is well suited to enable companies and research organizations to readily and cost effectively implement these R&D portfolio management systems.

A structured and proactive management of R&D portfolios is vital to develop-ing a strong innovation infrastructure to achieve both "fast failure" and "speed to market" with resultant higher project success rates.

3.6 Innovation Talent

A company or organization may have great technology and world class management systems but without top talent to execute, they will not be successful in the new, highly competitive world of innovation.

Gary Hamel in his book "The Future of Management" has warned that, in the next decade, companies will be challenged to change in a way that has no precedent. He also believes that most contemporary organizations do not have either "innovation DNA" or "adaptability DNA".

McKinsey partners, Lowell Bryan and Claudia Joyce, arrive at a similar conclusion in their book, "Mobilizing Minds" but from a slightly different perspective. They find that the 20th-century model of managing companies does not emphasize collaboration and wealth creation by talented employees but actually generates unnecessary complexity that works at cross-purposes to those critical goals.

Further, the Internet is making it possible to amplify and aggregate human capabilities in ways never before possible. But most CEOs don't yet understand how dramatically these developments will change the way companies organize, lead, allocate resources, plan, hire, and motivate – in other words, how new technology will change the work of managing.

New organizational models are needed in companies that engage in highly creative and innovative work. The traditional, hierarchically based 20th-century model is not effective at organizing the thinking-intensive work of self-directed people. These workers need to make subjective judgments based upon their own specialist knowledge and are increasingly self-directed and challenged as much by their peers as they are by their supervisors. Ideas are being monetized in ways never before possible, creating global wealth but also a more stimulating work environment, with more interesting jobs for employees to create more valuable products and services.

These are quite radical views which pose major challenges to the CEO's and senior management teams of more traditional companies that claim to have placed innovation at the top of their strategic agendas.

Knowledge-intensive talent is required for both the creative "idea generation" and the "speed to market" phases of the innovation process. The first phase might be described as "soft" management whereas the second phase might be more associated with a "hard" management style as shown in Fig. 3.9.

The type of person required for the "soft" phase will likely have a different profile from the typical person best suited for the "hard" phase of innovation management. A system for profiling professional workers, the so-called HAIR analysis, was developed some years ago in the Netherlands and has been successfully used by multinational companies. The human attributes of the HAIR profile include, helicopter (the ability to rise above detail), powers of analysis, imagination and sense of reality.

However, this HAIR profile analysis tends to be somewhat limited in the new global world of innovation, where other attributes such as teamwork, communication skills, interpersonal skills and leadership are also important and shown in Fig. 3.10.

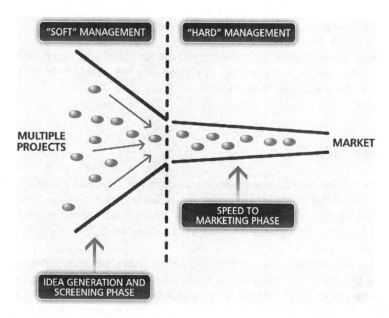

Fig. 3.9 "Soft" and "hard" innovation management phases (Author's drawing)

An ideal innovation team needs a balance of people skills required for the innovation process whereby for the "soft" phase, the skills of helicopter, analysis, imagination, communication, teamwork are important. For the "hard" phase of innovation, analysis and reality are the more prominent skills that need to be deployed although teamwork, leadership and communication skills are also highly valued. It is therefore important that managers appreciate these differences and create teams with the most suited skill sets for the different phases of the innovation process. This

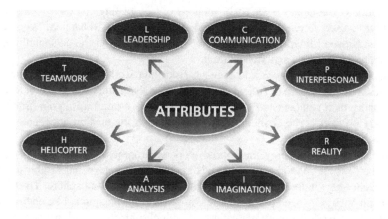

Fig. 3.10 Talent evaluation attributes (Author's drawing)

will not only improve the team outcomes but likely lead to a higher level of personal motivation from the team players.

Ideally, separate teams will be deployed for the "soft" and "hard" innovation phases with, perhaps, some overlap consisting of a few people with the unusual balance of skills across all these attributes.

3.7 Googleplex

A number of interesting new employee-management models are emerging from start-up companies often led by young senior management. Google, a relatively young and highly successful search engine and advertising company, offers a radical departure in innovation management achieved without the burden of a 20th century management structure.

Google was founded by Larry Page and Sergey Brin while they were students at Stanford University. The company was officially launched in September, 1998 in a friend's garage. In one of the most anticipated Initial Public Offerings (IPO), Google raised $1.67 billion in August of 2004. Today, Google has over 12,000 employees in offices throughout the world.

Google's mission statement and corporate culture reflect a philosophy that a company can "make money without doing evil" and that "work should be challenging and the challenge should be fun". These beliefs dominate life at Google. The official mission statement of the company is to "organize the world's information and make it universally accessible and useful." In 2006, Google was selected by MBA students as the ideal place to work and in 2007, Fortune Magazine named Google the Number 1 employer in their annual company review.

Google is highly committed to innovation and one big factor in their success is the company's willingness to accept that some projects fail. Google engineers are free to experiment with new features and new services and free to do so in public. The company frequently posts early versions of new features on their web site and waits for its users to react. "We can't predict exactly what will happen," says senior engineer, Nelson Minar. The cardinal rule at Google is, if you can do something that will improve the user's experience, do it.

The company also appears to manage risk quite well where good failures are "fast failures" according to Holzle at Google, who also emphasizes "fail before you invest more than you have to or before you needlessly compromise your brand with a shoddy product". The challenge lies in negotiating the tension between risk and caution.

Google is a high-energy, fast-paced work environment. While the dress code might be "casual", the company attracts and retains some of the brightest minds in the technology industry. There is a work hard, play hard atmosphere. The Google Mountain View, CA headquarters ("the Googleplex") is a campus-like environment with workout facilities, gourmet cafes and a highly informal working environment as shown in Fig. 3.11.

Fig. 3.11 A Googleplex office

All engineers at Google are encouraged to spend 20% of their work time on projects that interest them. Not only does this keep engineers happy and challenged, it is also good business as it is estimated that half of all new product launches can be directly attributed to projects that came from the 20%-time program.

Most workers at Google have base salaries that are on the lower end of the normal for this market but the remuneration is supplemented by stock options, challenging work and extensive benefits. In addition to the normal health and welfare benefits that larger companies offer, Google provides its employees with many additional cutting-edge benefits.

Teamwork is the norm, especially for big projects. Keith Coleman, a 26-year-old product manager who works on Gmail, oversees a ten-person secret project whose team members have taken over their own conference room. "They've given up their big space to be crammed into this room to get things done," says Google employee Coleman. The hideaway happens to be where Gmail's chat function was created. Lounge music is usually playing, engineers wander in and out, and there is no formal daily meeting, though the team tends to congregate between five and seven in the evening.

As Google continues to expand rapidly and globally, both organically and through recent acquisitions such as YouTube and DoubleClick, this will create new management challenges to disseminate, maintain and continue to evolve this innovative culture across a large multinational organization.

However, for well-established companies, the Google model is too radical and other innovation management approaches need to be adopted. It is vital that the personnel involved in the relatively high-risk innovation projects proactively receive full support from senior management. This is a common attribute found in all of the leading innovative companies around the world. The CEO's of these companies are continuously driving innovation as a top priority at all levels within the company.

It is likely that there will be a great deal of experimentation in the next 5–10 years, with both success and failure, as organizations search for the human talent management model in which innovation will thrive. The successful management and continued motivation of the new knowledge-intensive workforce will be challenging and there will be increasing global competition for this talent pool. It is also quite possible that different management models will emerge depending on whether the organization is primarily targeting incremental, quantum or disruptive innovation.

3.8 Entrepreneurs and Intrapreneurs

Senior management with strong entrepreneurial skills are a key component for the success of start-up companies. This skill ranks highly with venture capital companies when they are evaluating prospective investment proposals. Young companies are highly vulnerable to operational and strategic errors, hence the importance that is attached to early-stage management skills and experience.

Entrepreneurial talent needs to encompass all of the HAIR skills previously discussed as well as a strong drive to succeed in the face of numerous obstacles. The skills of imagination and sense of reality tend to be almost diametrically opposed, requiring an almost "schizophrenic" mind set to skillfully manage the innovation process.

The balanced management of risk is also a key component with start-up companies which often takes time to develop. Interestingly, in Silicon Valley, CEO's who have experienced some start-up failure as well as success, are highly valued for their exposure to risk management.

In large, well-established companies, management traditionally tends to be risk averse. This management characteristic, while valuable in the past, does not fit as well with the new increased emphasis on innovation which intrinsically carries a relatively high level of risk. Many multinationals are searching for ways to develop so-called intrapreneurial behaviour within the traditional hierarchical and conservative structure of a large company. Shell, the large multinational energy company, has created teams called "game changers" with the freedom and budget to explore new innovative ideas to drive future business growth. These intrapreneurial teams have had some success developing, for example, some quite novel approaches for deep sea oil and gas exploration and production.

Other companies such as 3M have, for many decades, created a strong and sustainable innovative culture throughout the organization. This culture is based on what 3M has defined as the "seven pillars of innovation" which comprise: management commitment to innovation; active maintenance of an innovative culture; broad-based technology innovation support; strong networking among researchers;

employee rewards for outstanding innovation achievements; quantifying revenue from new products over the past four years and ensuring that the research projects are tied to customer needs.

General Electric (GE), another large and diverse conglomerate, has created the buzz words "innovation = imagination" and is driving a culture of innovation forward across all their business sectors with cutting-edge technologies under development in areas such as photovoltaic power, wind power, medical devices and nanotechnology. The GE research facilities are also globally spread to be able to tap into innovative talent in rapidly developing countries such as India and China.

Hewlett Packard (HP) has also recently taken new initiatives to boost innovation and inspire engineers to turn concepts into products faster. The company launched an Innovation Program Office in 2006, with the goal of injecting small company entrepreneurial behaviour into the 156,000 employee company culture. The acquisition of a gaming company called, Voodoo, which has led to the development of the advanced HP Blackbird 002 PC product, has been an early direct outcome from this innovation initiative. This new PC has an elegant geometric design, a liquid cooling system and has features to support rich graphics. Other recent acquisitions, such as Snapfish, Tabblo and Flickr, are also aimed at stimulating innovation within HP by so-called "absorption".

3.9 Open Innovation

Companies such as Proctor & Gamble have adopted an "open innovation" policy whereby they are driving towards a goal of having some 50% of new products coming from early stage innovation outside their own company. In fact, the trend towards "open innovation" is gaining quite some momentum on a global scale. More and more companies are recognizing that there is a huge pool of creative talent outside their company that can be potentially tapped, particularly for the early "soft" phase of innovation.

Universities are an obvious target for companies seeking "open innovation" partnerships and this is indeed an increasing trend. The more entrepreneurial universities around the globe are embracing this new concept and adopting business models that facilitate the partnering with companies in early stage innovation. MIT in the US, for example, is very proactive and has formed innovation partnerships with a wide range of organizations and companies.

These include partnering with the Masdar project in the United Arab Emirates (UAE) to create a new research institute that will specialize in developing renewable technologies. This major project will also include a $250 million Clean Technology Fund and a special economic zone for the advanced energy industry. Another novel innovation management approach from MIT has been to form the Media Lab which focuses on human adaptability, including the human interaction with the computer which has led to the world renowned "One Laptop per Child" (OLPC) project. As more companies around the world adopt "open innovation", this will create opportunities for universities that embrace this business model to enjoy innovation partnerships that can offer attractive mutual benefits. In contrast, universities that, for various reasons, do not provide an attractive interface for these partnerships will likely not become part of this rapidly growing global innovation community.

Another approach to "open innovation" is where large corporations partner with small start-up companies who are highly innovative and develop new technology that could lead to new products or processes that have the potential to become part of their core business. Big pharma conglomerates have been partnering with small biotech companies for many years to create the opportunity to have the "first bite" at any new drugs that might emerge from these innovative yet risky start-ups.

The current global drive towards the development of renewable energy has led to a shift whereby multinational oil companies, who have traditionally had a more "closed innovation" policy, are now forming partnerships with small innovative companies in this field. Shell, for example, has formed a joint venture with HR Biopetroleum called "Cellana" to develop a demonstration facility to produce vegetable oil from marine algae that could provide a renewable feedstock for the production of biofuels. In addition, Shell has also formed a partnership with Iogen, a Canadian company, to develop an economically viable process to convert cellulosic biomass into fuel ethanol. Further embracing "open innovation", Shell has recently shifted strategy in their solar energy business by forming a joint venture with Saint Gobain Glass called "Avancis" to develop photovoltaic solar panels which are made using thin-film copper indium diselenide (CIS) technology. Their previous solar venture based on silicon panels has been divested in favour of the more advanced CIS technology.

Somewhat surprisingly, even automobile manufacturers, who in the past have not ventured into the fuels business, are now partnering with renewable-fuel start-up companies. General Motors has recently announced a partnership with Coskata, a relatively small innovative company that claims to have developed an advanced process to make ethanol cheaply from agricultural waste and even household garbage.

Many companies will increasingly realize that attempting to innovate in isolation is a risk they can no longer afford to take. The rapid diffusion of technology and

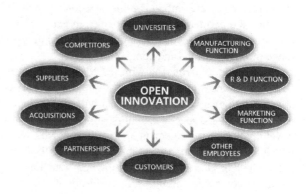

Fig. 3.12 The open innovation model (Author's drawing)

knowledge talent around the globe means that the "open innovation" model will be widely adopted in various forms. Many of the sources that can be tapped in relation to the open innovation model are shown in Fig. 3.12.

Tapping into this global innovation pool will therefore become increasingly important, which may make the traditional total ownership of IP an outmoded concept. The sharing of cutting-edge technology and portfolio management form the essential components of a new innovation paradigm that is essential for maximizing speed to market.

Chapter 4
Venture Innovation

Venture capital (VC) is a very powerful driver of quantum and disruptive innovation globally. Not only does venture capital simply provide funding but it also supports many of the other elements of the innovation process that are crucial to success. These may include technology due diligence, IP management, competitive analysis, business networking, operational management support, governance, financial discipline and marketing which is often, not always, fully recognized. Venture capital also provides a powerful market mechanism for "fast failure" innovation since a project that does not get VC funding will likely struggle for financing and therefore likely has a high risk profile. Overall, modern VC organizations have become very sophisticated at managing technical, managerial and financial risk, all of which is vitally important for a successful innovation process. In this regard, VC companies play a crucial role in providing relatively high-risk capital where other financial institutions dare not venture.

The very early stage of the innovation process is generally the most difficult to finance, more so since the bursting of the dot.com bubble in March, 2000. This led to a dramatic decrease in the availability of VC funding and following the more recent recovery period, VC companies have tended to shift their investment strategy further down the innovation value chain to reduce their risk. This trend has created an early-stage funding gap that is often filled by private angel investors, universities and government grants.

4.1 Sand Hill Road

The US leads the world in VC funding and Sand Hill Road, Menlo Park, in the heart of Silicon Valley, is the home to many big VC company names. Kleiner Perkins Caufield & Byers (KPCB), for example, has had phenomenal past success having backed companies such as Amazon, Genentech, Google and Sun Microsystems in their early days. For several years during the dotcom boom of the late 1990s, commercial real estate on Sand Hill Road was more expensive than almost anywhere else in the world. Other notable VC companies in this area include Matrix Partners, Sequoia Capital, TPG Capital, Venrock, Kohlberg Kravis Roberts and US Venture

I.E. Maxwell, *Managing Sustainable Innovation*,
DOI 10.1007/978-0-387-87581-1_4, © 2009 by Ian E. Maxwell

Partners. Some smaller, early-stage biotech VC's such as 5AM Ventures are also located along this famous Silicon Valley road.

4.2 Global Venture Capitalists

Venture Capital is now becoming a global business and a number of major US companies have expanded their market presence and opened offices abroad. For example, Sequoia Capital, which has funded companies such as, Cisco Systems, Oracle and Apple, has offices in China, India and Israel. IDG Ventures, another global VC player with approximately \$3.7 billion under management, has offices in Boston, San Francisco, India, Korea, China and Vietnam. KPCB also has offices in Beijing and Shanghai reflecting the growing importance of China as a source of innovation and entrepreneurship. Interestingly, the most active venture capital investors in China in 2006 were IDG Ventures China and Sequoia Capital.

As these large US-based VC companies enter these emerging markets, they will not only provide early stage capital but also valuable management expertise to stimulate and support innovation and entrepreneurship in these rapidly growing economies.

4.3 University Seed Funds

The commercialization of IP has become popular with universities around the world but they often struggle with early-stage funding. This has triggered many universities to develop their own venture capital funds or to form partnerships with large financial investment companies willing to allocate a small percentage of their funds to a higher risk asset class.

For example, in 2000, a group of Australian universities, Queensland, Melbourne and New South Wales, formed a seed-stage venture capital fund called Uniseed, to commercialize innovative ideas based on their research output. The early success of this fund, particularly in the biotech sector, has led to expansion involving Westscheme, a Western Australian superannuation fund. Strong links into the Silicon Valley network have enabled many of the Uniseed-funded university spin-outs to gain later stage funding from US venture capital companies.

In the UK, the Cambridge Enterprise Seed Funds were established in 2000, as part of a network of such funds at the leading universities of UK. A partnership comprising the Cambridge University Office of Science and Technology, the Wellcome Trust and the Gatsby Charitable Foundation committed £50 million to establish the first University Challenge Funds with the aim of "assisting the successful transformation of good research into good business".

The Seed Funds offer finance at the high-risk early stage of a business with a range of funding levels including:

- Pathfinder funding of up to £10 K for carrying out market and Intellectual Property assessments, planning marketing strategies.
- Concept funding of up to £80 K which can be used for applied development to prove a concept and assess the market.
- Seed funding of up to £250 K for setting up a joint venture or partnership.

The Seed Funds invest across all technologies and have invested in a portfolio of over twenty companies, more than 50% of which are based on life science technology or target healthcare applications.

Numerous universities in the US have established early stage venture funds. For example, the University Venture Fund (UVF) is an independent fund that leverages the innovations of students from around the country. The fund is a form of collaboration between students seeking an entrepreneurial education and professional venture capitalists to search out high-tech and consumer trends with potential. The UVF comprises graduate and undergraduate student associates from the University of Utah, Brigham Young University, Westminster College in Salt Lake City, as well as the Wharton School of Business at the University of Pennsylvania, and Stanford University. The program attracts students interested in start-ups and immerses them in an environment that allows them to identify and connect with prospects that may otherwise go unnoticed by the venture capital world. Students also perform extensive due diligence research evaluating technologies, finances, management teams and marketing strategies of companies. This process not only provides value to the Fund and its partners, but also provides a well-rounded entrepreneurship education to the students.

Chinese universities are also starting to form VC entities with the goal of commercializing IP and stimulating innovation. For example, in 2001 the top-tier, Tsinghua University in Beijing has established its own venture capital fund, Tsing Capital with a focus on clean technology.

4.4 Strategic Venture Capital

Many large companies have formed their own venture capital groups as a vehicle for gaining access to emerging technologies with the potential to be future core-business opportunities. Pharmaceutical giants such as Pfizer and GSK have had their own venture funds for some time in order to be able to scan the markets for interesting new biotech investment opportunities. These majors offer not only capital but insights into drug markets and are, therefore, attractive venture capital investors for small companies. Furthermore, strategic investors provide significant credibility for a new company towards financial co-investors and potential customers.

For example, both Pfizer and GSK invested in Avantium, a high throughput process technology company, founded by the author, and brought a wealth of knowledge about the future needs of the drug-manufacturing industry into the fledgling company. These companies also funded contract research in Avantium which provided a valuable source of early-stage revenues.

In industries other than pharmaceuticals, large companies are also establishing venture funds to provide early access to new innovations. Examples across a wide range of business sectors include Proctor and Gamble, Cisco, Microsoft, Google, Intel, Motorola, Johnson & Johnson, Novartis, Siemens, Shell, BP, Nestle and many other large multinationals.

4.5 Clean Energy Technology Venturing

Inherent in the nature of venture-capital companies is their concentration on the newest "hot" emerging technologies. In recent years, they have invested in biotechnology, medical devices, nanotechnology and the internet. However, particularly in the US, clean and renewable energy is rapidly becoming the most attractive prospect. The global energy business is massive in scale with a value of $6 trillion per year and underpins global economic growth. The recent dramatic peak in the price of crude oil together with growing concerns about global warming and rising pollution have created a strong focus on clean energy technologies.

These mega trends have triggered a number of high profile VC companies to decide that clean energy is the "next big thing" and they have created new funds to focus on innovative technologies that are both non-polluting and break the global dependence on fossil fuels. In Silicon Valley alone, the VC investment in clean energy has risen astronomically from $250 million in 2005 to $1.2 billion in 2007, with energy generation and transportation fuels absorbing most of this funding.

Vinod Khosla, a successful co-founder of Sun Microsystems, formed a new fund in 2004 called Khosla Ventures, which is based in Menlo Park and focused on clean and renewable energy. Khosla Ventures invests in companies that meet the following criteria:

- Tackle practical and manageable problems.
- Technologies that can achieve unsubsidized market competitiveness within 5–7 years.
- Technologies that have the potential to scale up significantly with decreasing unit costs.
- Technologies that have manageable start-up costs and short innovation cycles.

To date, Khosla Ventures has invested in some 30 companies that include: Stion that is developing thin-film solar cells; Segetis that is targeting to convert biomass into high added value speciality chemicals; LS9 and Amyris Biotechnology that is using enzymatic processes to convert biomass into biofuel; and Range Fuels that converts cellulosic waste biomass into synthesis gas which is further processed into ethanol.

All of the biofuels investments are required to meet a further set of so-called CLAW criteria:

C – **C**ost below gasoline.
L – **L**ow to no additional land use.
A – **A**ir quality improvements (i.e. low carbon emissions).
W – Limited **W**ater use.

Khosla has a vision of replacing the current massive crude oil based refineries with a much larger number of smaller bio-refineries located near the sources of renewable biomass feedstock.

Other VC's active in this area include KPCB, which has established a $500 million fund focused on investment in "green" technologies, while Al Gores's Generation Investment Management has raised nearly $ 700 million for a "climate solutions" fund. An important characteristic of clean technology investments, unlike IT investments for example, is that they require large amounts of capital to build manufacturing processes before they can produce products and become profitable. This has prompted these VC companies to seek new types of partners for later-stage investments who have access to very large sums of capital.

Notably, traditional energy conglomerates that have, in the past, shied away from early-stage venturing are starting to co-invest, together with VC companies, in promising renewable energy start-up companies. BP and Shell are prominent in this regard, investing in solar energy and biofuels companies, recognizing that these emerging technologies will play an increasing role in the energy business of the future. More specifically, Shell has invested in Cellena, a Hawaiian algae-to-biofuel start-up, and is working with Codexis and Iogen, two young companies developing technology based on enzymes to convert cellulosic biomass to fuels. BP has decided to back Craig Venter's start-up company, Synthetic Genomics, that has the highly ambitious target of synthesizing the genome of an enzyme that will convert carbon dioxide into hydrocarbon fuels, and within a remarkably short time scale, developing a commercially viable process based on this technology. Somewhat more conservatively, BP has also recently announced a foray into Brazil's sugarcane-based ethanol industry by taking a 50% stake in Tropical BioEnergia.

4.6 US Venture Capital

The US leads the world by a large margin in numbers of venture capital funds and volume of investment, which is a major catalyst for innovation in this country. According to Dow Jones, venture capital investments in the US reached an all time peak of $83 billion in the year 2000 before the dotcom bubble burst. After plummeting to about $10 billion in 2003, there has since been a slow recovery to a level of $24 billion in 2006 as shown in Fig. 4.1.

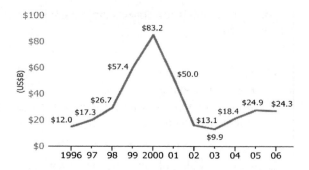

Fig. 4.1 US venture capital investments (1996–2006) (Source: Venture Capital Industry Report, Dow Jones, 2007; redrawn)

However, since the investment peak in 2000, the average fund size has doubled from around $100 to $200 million, possibly reflecting higher overhead costs. The San Francisco Bay area continues to dominate geographically, generating some 35% of US venture capital activity in 2006. The major business areas of venture capital investment over the past five years have been IT and healthcare. However, it is conceivable, given the current rapid growth in clean and renewable energy funding, and the high levels of investment required for commercialization of the technology, that this business sector could potentially grow to dominate venture capital in the US within a few years.

4.7 European Venture Capital

Compared with the US, the levels of venture capital in Europe are relatively low, reaching only $4.1 billion in 2006. As in the US, the IT and healthcare sectors were the dominant areas for venture capital funding. Clearly, to drive innovation forward and compete with the US, Europe needs to stimulate much higher levels of venture capital investment.

4.8 Israeli Venture Capital

Israel has a remarkably high level of venture capital investment, given the relatively small population of the country, reaching $1.4 billion in 2006 and $1.8 billion in 2007. This strong risk capital funding underpins the rapid growth of the knowledge-based sector of the economy in Israel. In fact, the technology parks in Israel are often dubbed "Silicon Wadis" reflecting their resemblance to Silicon Valley in the US. Perhaps not surprisingly, defence-related technology, in addition to IT and healthcare, is a leading component of the Israeli high tech sector.

4.9 Chinese Venture Capital

Venture capital in mainland China has experienced significant growth in 2006, reaching a level of $1.9 billion which represents a 55% increase from the previous year. The strong inflows of capital into China and the government drive to stimulate technology commercialization should ensure that venture capital will continue to grow strongly in the coming years. The rate of this expansion of risk capital will play an important role in determining how rapidly China can move the economy from a low-cost manufacturing base to becoming a significant player in the high-end global knowledge arena.

Venture capital is a vital element of the innovation infrastructure and governments should strive to create a financial environment in which this risk capital will flourish. This includes a favourable tax structure, flexible employment policies, share option schemes, robust IP legislation, balanced bankruptcy laws and even co-funding of the high-risk, early stage of start-up companies. Despite the global growth of venture capital, the US remains dominant and will continue to enjoy a significant competitive advantage in this regard in the foreseeable future.

Chapter 5
Academic Innovation

Academic innovation may seem like a contradiction in terms, but as governments around the world steadily withdraw their financial support, cash-starved universities are racing to generate income through the commercialization of their intellectual property (IP). This IP, which is mainly captured in the form of patents, has been harvested from the university research activities. Many governments are encouraging this shift towards innovation at universities in the hope of creating another "Silicon Valley" to stimulate high added value economic activity.

The Bayh-Doyle Act of 1980 was a landmark piece of legislation in the US and unlocked all inventions and discoveries that had been funded throughout the US with taxpayers' money. This Act which has been termed the "Innovation's Golden Goose" was instrumental in encouraging universities to commercialize their IP.

In order to more effectively manage these commercially oriented activities alongside their traditional academic roles, universities around the world have formed so-called technology transfer offices (TTOs). While there are many major success stories, the conversion of IP into significant revenue streams inside an academic environment can be very challenging and is characterized by long lead times.

5.1 Success Stories

MIT, Stanford University, Caltech, Johns Hopkins, Harvard and the University of California campuses, with their large research budgets and world class research teams, tend to dominate the IP success rankings.

However, some smaller US universities also have their success stories such as the sport drink, Gatorade, which was developed at the University of Florida and earns $9 million per year in trade mark licensing fees from the Pepsi Cola Company. This university has continued to innovate and now earns some $20 million in licensing fees per year from the pharmaceutical company, Merck, for a glaucoma drug called Trusopt. Royalty and licensing income for the University of Florida now exceeds some $40 million per annum.

I.E. Maxwell, *Managing Sustainable Innovation*,
DOI 10.1007/978-0-387-87581-1_5, © 2009 by Ian E. Maxwell

Florida State University (FSU) can also claim fame for their early stage development of the blockbuster cancer drug, Taxol. It was the determination of Professor Holton at FSU that led to a successful synthesis of Taxol using compounds found in the needles and twigs of the common English Yew tree. This semi-synthetic route enabled Taxol to be produced in sufficient quantities to be widely used as a major chemotherapy for breast and ovarian cancer. The pharmaceutical giant, Bristol Myers Squid, funded the clinical trials and took Taxol to market and paid FSU some $200 million in royalties through the 1990s.

Stanford University computer science students, Larry Page and Sergey Brin, developed an algorithm for web searching that led to formation of the now legendary IT giant, Google. The two students had the insight to recognize that web searching could be greatly improved if dual criteria of importance and relevance were used. For a particular query, the importance of a web site was determined by the number of web sites that link to it and the relevance was determined if the content of the web site and the content of other web sites that link to it match the query. This brilliant algorithm was patented by the Stanford University Office of Technology and Licensing and later given the trade name PageRank. In 2004, following the highly successful initial public offering (IPO) on the NASDAQ in 2004, Stanford University reputedly sold their shares in Google for some $320 million.

Another major success story is the development of the nicotine patch that was initially developed at the University of California at Los Angeles (UCLA). This highly successful skin patch transmitted low doses of nicotine into the bloodstream and thereby enabled many people to break the habit of smoking. The development of the patch took many years of testing with support from the Swiss pharmaceutical company, Ciba Geigy. This technology has assisted many thousands of people to quit smoking with enormous benefit in terms of human health and medical costs.

5.2 Research and Technology Commercialization

The commercial activities of university TTOs often include the licensing of IP, contract research and spin-out companies. As might be expected, the generation of IP tends to track the level and quality of research carried out by the university. Further, although the financial data tends to be scarce, there does appear to be a correlation between the research expenditure and TTO commercialization revenues (excluding contract research revenue) as shown in Fig. 5.1.

Other commercialization measurements, such as number of patents, licensing deals and start-up companies per year also tend to broadly track total research expenditure. Major one-off success stories such as the Google IPO for Stanford University, generate annual revenues for particular years that fall well outside these general trends.

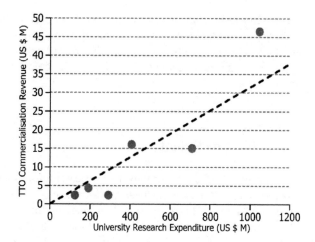

Fig. 5.1 University IP commercialization revenue and research expenditure (Author's drawing)

5.3   License or Spin-Out

Universities are often faced with the issue of deciding whether to monetize IP by licensing the technology or forming a spin-out company. The former strategy is lower risk and often yields a faster flow of revenue but the up-side is generally considerably less than that of a successful spin-out company.

An example of a spin-out is provided by the author's direct experience in 2001 of forming a new company based on technology developed within a Dutch university research environment. Professor Jan-Pieter Abrahams of Leiden University and the author developed a high throughput drug polymorph (different crystalline forms of the same drug molecule) screening technology using miniaturized, automated crystallization and analysis techniques. This technique enabled drug polymorphs to be rapidly determined using minute amounts of material. The identification of such polymorphs is crucial for defining the manufacturing process for a drug and for the FDA approval procedures. In addition, since patents may be granted for different drug polymorphs, their identification is a key element of the drug discovery and patent protection program for many biotech and pharmaceutical companies. A new start-up company was launched in 2001, called Crystallics, based on this rapid screening technology achieving financial break-even within only 18 months of operation.

Another interesting example of university licensing involves the development of a new lithium-ion battery based on technology developed a few years ago at MIT in the US. Professor Yet-Ming Chiang at MIT developed extremely thin layers of nano lithium phosphate that dramatically improves the performance of lithium-ion batteries. These new generation batteries have double the power density and discharge and regenerate very rapidly compared to conventional batteries. A new company called A123 was formed in 2001 to exploit this innovation and licensed the technology from MIT. This start-up company has been very successful in attracting some \$250 million in funding from both high-profile venture capital companies, such as Sequoia Capital, as well as strategic investors such as GE and Duracell. In addition, A123 is already moving rapidly forward with a broad range of commercial applications for their new batteries which include power tools, plug-in electric cars and utility storage.

5.4 Publish or Patent

Not surprisingly, the top-tier university research groups tend to be the source of the most valuable IP. However, these research teams are keen to publish research in prestigious journals and to present their latest findings at International conferences. Moreover, governments around the world are introducing systems to measure the performance of their academic staff in which the number of publications in major international journals is a key contributing factor.

The above drivers tend to make university researchers reluctant to delay publications and take the time and effort to develop the basis for a robust patent. This delay in publication is a key part of the patenting process since any material that has been published in the open literature is considered to be "prior art" and will invalidate any patent application.

Successful university TTOs have developed organizational structures and processes to enable top-tier academic research to flourish alongside the capturing and bringing to market of the valuable IP generated by these teams.

5.5 Valley of Death

Another major hurdle for universities is to nurture their IP to a stage whereby external investors, such as venture capital companies, will provide the funding and the management support required to drive the innovation process to market. This gap between the academic early-stage IP and external funding is often referred to as the "valley of death" where many projects fail through lack of finance, creating an innovation "choke point" as shown in Fig. 5.2.

As governments increasingly recognize the importance of innovation for GDP growth and this new innovation role of universities, they are addressing this "valley of death" problem. A number of approaches have been taken that involve the governments providing co-funding under attractive terms to reduce the risk and attract external investors into this early stage of the innovation process. In addition, a number of university TTOs have set up their own early-stage venture capital funds. However, it is not only lack of finance that may act as an innovation blocker, since universities also often lack the resources and skills to focus on this early stage of commercialization. This has led to the development of so-called incubators and technology parks to provide a bridge to commerce.

Fig. 5.2 The Innovation "Valley of Death" (Author's drawing)

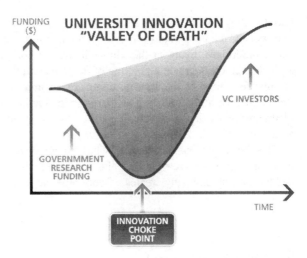

5.6 University Innovation Governance

The governance of innovation is possibly the greatest blocker or stimulus for innovation within a university environment. The dilemma facing university administrators is that there is, in general, not a good match between the ideal academic and innovation cultures.

One solution to this problem is to create a TTO governance structure that has a significant degree of independence from the university administration. This can be achieved by creating the TTO as a separate legal entity and with its own board, management and employees. This TTO entity can be fully owned by the university but has the freedom to act as a separate commercial organization and create a culture in which innovation can thrive alongside academia.

In such a governance structure, the link back to the university management can be through participation in the TTO board. A number of universities around the world have successfully adopted this TTO governance model.

For example, Auckland UniServices, the commercial arm of Auckland University in New Zealand, has pioneered this governance model and has achieved remarkable revenue growth of some 15–20% per year over a period of some 20 years. This TTO now provides approximately 50% of all the externally funded research that is carried out at Auckland University. The highly valued research is contracted to UniServices by both local and overseas industry, government ministries and their own start-up companies. This TTO boost to research at Auckland University has undoubtedly contributed to the considerable achievement of being ranked among the top 50 universities in the world.

The attractiveness of this element of the TTO business model, forming start-up companies that provide high-quality research back into the university, is that the benefits are immediate even though the potential royalties, milestone payments or share liquidity may take many years to materialize. In effect, this is a mechanism for a university to capture venture capital funding for research. In the case of Auckland UniServices, many of their biotech start-up companies are funding research at the university to create a pipeline of drugs behind the lead drug that enabled the original formation of the start-up company. Examples include companies such as Proacta, which has a lead drug and strong pipeline in cancer therapies, and Neuren Pharmaceuticals that is developing drugs for brain injury and neurodegeneration treatment.

This innovation business model, when executed well, is a win for all parties: the university gains research funding; the TTO gains revenues and a management fee; and the start-up company creates a future pipeline of drugs.

5.7 Enterprise Centres

An interesting approach to the academic innovation dilemma is a so-called enterprise centres governance model that involves the formation of commercialization centres that are devolved from the central TTO and spread strategically around the university campus as shown in Fig. 5.3.

These enterprise centres provide a local commercial interface with the university centres of research excellence. This model, when executed properly, enables the TTO commercialization teams to interact closely with the relevant research groups providing an innovative stimulus without damaging the quality of the academic research. Each enterprise centre may be given its own financial goals which could

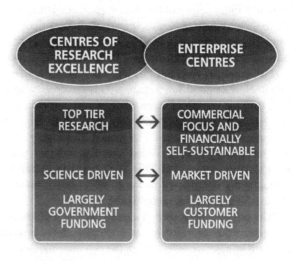

Fig. 5.3 University TTO enterprise centres (Author's drawing)

require it to become financially self-sustaining within a 3–5 year period. Another advantage of this approach is that it prevents the TTO centre from becoming too large and distant from the research activities of the university. Auckland UniServices, the progressive TTO of the University of Auckland in New Zealand, has successfully developed this devolved enterprise centre model to enhance both contract research and IP commercialization.

5.8 AUTM

The Association of University Technology Managers (AUTM) is a non-profit professional US based association with a mission to advance the field of technology transfer. AUTM has some 3,600 members representing the TTO managers from more than 350 universities, research institutions, teaching hospitals and government agencies, as well as hundreds of companies involved with managing and licensing innovations derived from academic and non-profit research. This organization is very active in sharing knowledge and best practices related to technology transfer.

In 2005, AUTM launched the "Better World Project" to promote public understanding of how academic research and technology transfer have changed our way of life and made the world a better place. The project draws from more than a decade of case studies from their members. It is intended to produce ongoing reports to provide a greater awareness of how public funded research has led to major advances in areas such as healthcare, IT and innovative products and services. These reports are now produced biannually and provide an excellent update on examples of successful university technology transfer either in the form of licensing or start-up companies.

5.9 Science and Technology Parks

Many countries have stimulated the development of science and technology parks (STPs) inside or adjacent to universities, often with the prime aim of enhancing innovation through closer interaction between academic research and business. These STPs often encompass an incubator facility to provide support services to fledgling science-based companies at low cost. STPs have now become an established part of the innovation infrastructure that is particularly well suited to developing knowledge-based economies.

The Twente STP in the Netherlands is a melting pot of innovative activities where "science" as well as "business" profit from each other, technologically as well as commercially. The successful formula is perceived to result from a unique location, outstanding facilities, an intensive and active knowledge exchange, and an atmosphere that encourages mutual beneficial cooperation. The combination of university study, high tech knowledge-based industry, and business services generates both ideas and jobs and has proven to be a very strong magnet for like-minded companies and investors. This STP has grown to create a large innovation ecosystem encompassing some 200 knowledge-intensive companies employing about 4,000 people. This success can most likely be attributed to the strong entrepreneurial culture of the partnering technical university.

The Biopolis was a $1 billion mega project funded by the Singapore government to create a world class biomedical innovation ecosystem. This STP, which is highly research oriented, is close to the National University of Singapore, the Singapore Polytechnic, the Institute of Technical Education, the National University Hospital and the Singapore Science Park. The campus is dedicated to providing the infrastructure for research and development activities and promoting peer review and collaboration among the private and public scientific community with the ambition of becoming the biomedical hub of Asia.

In the Waikato region, the centre of the booming dairy industry in New Zealand, an Innovation Park has been set up to bring together and maximize the synergy between both small and large companies in the agriculture and biotechnology areas. The concept of a thematic innovation park and the close interaction with Waikato University has been successful in creating a high technology hub for this important sector of the New Zealand economy. Waikato Link, the highly successful commercial arm of Waikato University, is also located within this innovation park as well as a number of their start-up companies.

The success of STPs seems to vary widely depending on how well they contribute to catalyse the formation of an innovation ecosystem. Clearly, the entrepreneurial profile of the adjoining university will play a key role in providing a dynamic interface with the STP. The inherent risk associated with investing in STPs is that they turn into a pure "real estate play" and do not foster innovation as originally envisaged.

5.10 Entrepreneurial University Ecosystems

In high-growth economies in the developing world, where dedicated technological institutes are being established to provide a cadre of graduates for the high-tech economy, the opportunity exists to integrate the various elements described above into an entrepreneurial university ecosystem, as indicated in Fig. 5.4.

The basic research required to underpin top-tier science and technology skill pools would be provided on the basis of national competitive bidding, through government granting channels. The university would also possibly contribute to this basic research funding from educational profits, endowment funds and other external sources.

Central funds would be concentrated on well-defined centres of research excellence, where the university has been able to achieve a critical mass of researchers with world-class infrastructure and skills. The specialized teaching and training staff required by the university would be drawn from these centres.

The university technology transfer office (TTO) would be set up as a separate legal entity with its own board and executive team to both develop a strong

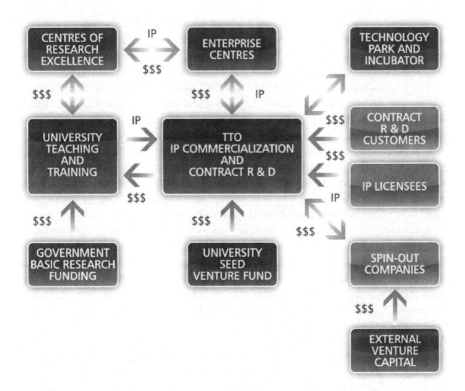

Fig. 5.4 A model entrepreneurial university ecosystem (Author's drawing)

commercial culture and create the dynamism required of a modern, high-technology, globally oriented business. The IP developed from the university research would be owned and managed by the TTO which would include funding and supporting all of the related patent and copyright activities.

To avoid creating a large central TTO organization that becomes distant from both the university researchers and the needs of external customers, a system of devolved enterprise centres specializing in various business sectors could be developed. Ideally, these enterprise centres will be physically located near the centres of research excellence that match with the research skills required to support their sector of the business. Each enterprise centre will operate as a separate business unit under the governance structure of the TTO with its own financial and IP generation targets.

In addition, the TTO would govern and manage a technology park and incubator that would attract high-technology companies to collaborate closely with the research centres of excellence and the relevant enterprise centre. The incubation facilities and management support would be provided to the TTO spin-out companies at low cost to enhance the chance of success. These fledgling companies would also enjoy financial support from the university early stage venture fund. Follow-on investments in the start-up companies would be provided from a trusted network of external VC organizations. The start-up companies and their investors would be encouraged to contract research back into the university, where possible, to provide new sources of research funding and thereby enhance the entrepreneurial ecosystem.

The revenue-generating activities of the TTO would come from multiple sources that would include contract R&D from external organizations and companies, license fees from IP agreements, research agreements and equity liquidation from spin-out companies, and income derived from the technology park and incubator.

It is proposed that such an entrepreneurial university provides a better fit with a modern, knowledge-based economy where the integration of science, technology and business is becoming so vital to success. Students that are both educated and trained in research within such an entrepreneurial ecosystem will be well suited and qualified to enter the new knowledge-based economy workforce.

Some elements of this entrepreneurial structure can, of course, already be found in many universities around the world. In established institutions, governance structures and tradition are often such that the interfaces between the academic research and commercialization activities create unnecessarily high levels of friction and there may be understandable resistance to the adoption of such an entrepreneurial system. Dedicated technological institutes are likely to be more enthusiastic than universities offering both traditional programs and cutting-edge science and technology. However, for the latter also, the case can be made that the presence of an integrated entrepreneurial system as outlined can be beneficial; since it is potentially self-financing, it need no longer compete with the institution's other programs for scarce funds. For emerging economies where new technological universities are being created, this entrepreneurial model could potentially provide a dynamic education, training, research and high-technology ecosystem that could provide a cornerstone to the infrastructure required to foster a thriving, knowledge-based economy.

Chapter 6
Innovative China

The last decade has seen the rise of large emerging economies such as China and India to the status of global players. China has enjoyed dramatic double-digit GDP growth during this period driven by providing the world with low-cost manufacturing capabilities. However, China is now demonstrating the ambition to "lift the game" and develop its own IP and global brands by providing a strong stimulus for innovation.

6.1 Inventive to Innovative Dragons

China has a long history of notable inventions including silk weaving, the magnetic compass, astronomical clocks, suspension bridges, gun powder, hydraulics and iron smelting. Somewhat surprisingly, China lost this early technological lead to Europe in the 15th century because the country was unable to capitalize on these inventions to create an innovation-driven economy. According to Denis Simon of the Levin Graduate Institute, this was most likely due to the fact that these early Chinese inventors were artisans and craftsman and were unable to influence the governing by scholar bureaucrats who were preoccupied with philosophical and moral issues.

Today, China is the world's largest technocracy: a country ruled largely by scientists and engineers who believe in the power of new technologies to deliver social and economic progress. Furthermore, having now embraced a market-driven economy, there is a clear intent from the Chinese government to leverage their scientific and technological strengths to drive innovation. While the Chinese innovation system has its weaknesses, it does, however, excel at the rapid mobilization of resources.

The rate of adoption of the Internet in China is also staggering. At the Seventh China Hi-Tech Trade Fair held recently in Shenzhen, Ministry of Information Vice-Minister, Lou Qinjian, announced that, as of September 2007, China had 172 million Internet users. This figure indicates that in 2007, approximately 4 million Chinese people went online for the first time every month.

I.E. Maxwell, *Managing Sustainable Innovation*,
DOI 10.1007/978-0-387-87581-1_6, © 2009 by Ian E. Maxwell

6.2 Chinese Science and Technology

The indispensability of world-class science and technology, as a foundation for economic growth in the new knowledge-based global economy, has been well recognized by the Chinese government. This strategy is reflected in a keynote speech in 2006 to the Chinese Congress by President Hu Jintao, who called on China to become an "innovation-oriented society". He also proposed that "by the end of 2020, China will achieve many science and technology breakthroughs of great world influence, qualifying it to join the ranks of the world's most innovative countries". Recent visits by the author to Chinese top-tier universities and research institutes have served to reinforce the view that China has indeed the potential to become a significant player in the new global innovation race.

However, the path from scientific research to the commercialization of technology is complex, involving many phases often associated with high levels of technical and financial risk. Hence, in addition to this substantial investment in science and technology, there will also need to be significant investment in training and support to develop the specialized skills to transform the research achievements into commercially viable products and services suited for both local and world markets.

It has also been suggested that the Confucian values system may be an obstacle to innovation in present-day China, because this system discourages challenges to authority and unconventional thinking. However, many professors at top universities and research managers believe that Chinese society is changing rapidly such that these Confucian values are no longer a significant barrier to innovation.

6.3 Planning for 15 Years Ahead

In early 2006, China announced a 15-year plan to boost science, technology and innovation with the long-term goal of becoming a pre-eminent global economic and technological power. This is reflected in a rapid growth in R&D spending in China during the last decade as shown Fig. 6.1.

The Chinese government leaders are planning to further increase research and development spending from the current level of 1.3% of GDP to 2.0% by 2010 and 2.5% by 2020. This plan is targeting for science and technology to account for some 60% of economic growth and for China to be among the top five countries worldwide in terms of patents and scientific citations. The following sectors have been identified as key areas of investment for the 15-year period to realize the science and technology plan as shown in Fig. 6.2.

6.4 The Chinese Academy of Sciences

The Chinese Academy of Sciences (CAS) was formed in 1949 and is the most prestigious science organization in China. It employs some 100,000 researchers, making

Fig. 6.1 Rapid growth in
China R&D spending
(redrawn from source)

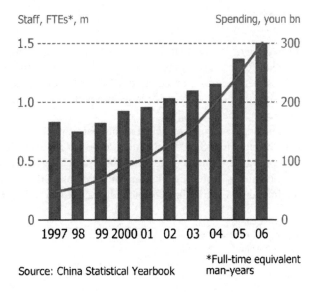

Source: China Statistical Yearbook

*Full-time equivalent
man-years

Fig. 6.2 The China 15-year
science and technology
priorities (Author's drawing)

**China's 15 Year Science and Technology Priorities
(2006-2020)**

Advanced Storage Technologies
Alternative and Renewable Energies
Biotechnology/Genetics
Electronic Components
Environmental Technologies
Integrated Circuits/Semiconductors
Manned Space Exploration
Materials Technology
Nanotechnology
Network and Communication Technologies
Optical and Biological Computing
Software and Related Services

it one of the largest research organizations in the world. By 2010, CAS will have
about 80 national institutes noted for their powerful capacities in science, technology, innovation and sustainable development. In recent years, there has been a strong
emphasis within CAS to deploy the science and technology base to foster innovation
and contribute to knowledge-based economic growth.

Interestingly, the CAS organization also has its own graduate university
(GUCAS) with five campuses in the Beijing region and some 30,000 students, half
of whom are studying at PhD level.

6.5 IP Issues

Protection of intellectual property (IP) rights is currently a significant shortcoming but the Chinese government has recently made significant strides forward in both the legislation and enforcement of IP. Clearly, it will take some time to both educate and shift the culture of such a large and populous country to both develop their own and respect the IP of others.

China has recently launched an annual "patent week" to promote patent protection through their State Intellectual Property Office (SIPO). During this week, trade fairs, exhibitions and lectures take place in Beijing and about 20 other provinces and municipalities including Tianjin, Shanghai and Jilin. The filing of Chinese patent applications is increasing exponentially as shown in Fig. 6.3.

Fig. 6.3 Growth in Chinese patents (Author's drawing)

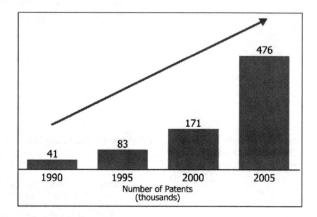

Now that China has important World Trade Organization commitments and given the potential for damage to its own developing Chinese industries, it is clearly in China's interests to enforce intellectual property (IP) rights. With newly enacted laws, China has been steadily improving and increasing their enforcement of IP rights in a non-biased manner.

Registration of IP in China is important and should be done promptly so that rights can be enforced when needed. Many multinational companies are now including China in their foreign filing patent portfolio.

6.6 University Technology Commercialization and Collaboration

Chinese universities are also rapidly adopting the western model whereby universities are forming separate technology transfer office entities to commercialize technology emerging from their own research.

Tsinghua International Technology Transfer Center (ITTC) is a good example where they not only commercialize the technology developed by Tsinghua University but also assist foreign universities and companies to enter the Chinese market. For example, Tsinghua ITTC hosted a Technology Networking Forum in April 2008 between New Zealand and China, aimed at building relationships and enhancing collaboration in the field of innovation and technology commercialization.

United Kingdom (UK) universities are also proactively engaging with their Chinese counterparts and a new Innovation China UK (ICUK) programme was launched in November, 2007, to promote joint innovation and knowledge transfer between the two countries. ICUK, involving five British and more than 10 Chinese higher education institutions (HEIs), supports academic and business partners in forging collaborations, funding proof-of-concept research and commercializing joint intellectual property across the UK and China.

The ICUK will focus its main activities on energy, climate change and sustainable environment, infectious diseases, biomedicine and drug discovery (including traditional Chinese medicine), nanotechnology and material science, and space technology. These knowledge bases are prioritized as key collaboration areas by the UK and China.

The UK is providing £5 million funding from the Higher Education Innovation Fund which supports knowledge transfer and increased business engagement in universities. China is providing complementary funding through its Ministry of Science and Technology. The British ICUK partners are Queen Mary University, the University of London (lead institution), King's College London, the University of Nottingham, the Royal Veterinary College, and the University of Southampton.

The ICUK Chinese collaborators include the Chinese Academy of Science (over five institutes), Tsinghua University, Beijing University of Aerospace and Aeronautics, Fudan University, Shanghai Jiaotong University, China Ocean University, Nanjing University, University of Science and Technology China and Xi'an Jiaotong University.

6.7 TORCH

The organization called TORCH is a subsidiary of the Ministry of Science and Technology (MOST) and is the sole agency commissioned by the Ministry to improve the overall environment for innovation and high-tech industry development. As in the West, high-technology parks are being actively promoted by TORCH in China. The growth in revenue generated from these parks during the last decade has been phenomenal, reaching some $110 billion in 2005.

More importantly, the TORCH organization also supports the development of sector-specific Technology Business Incubators (TBIs) of which there are now 62. These incubators are located next to universities such as Tsinghua University, Shanghai Jiaotong University, Tongji University, Chongqing University and Sichuan

University. Nine international business incubators have also been established to accommodate foreign start-ups.

Sector-specific TBIs that have recently been formed include the following:

- Shanghai Zhangjiang Bio-Medicine Incubator.
- Beijing Medical University Incubator.
- Beijing Internal Combustion Engine Manufacture Incubation Base.
- Beijing Advanced Material Incubator.
- Shanxi Yangling Agricultural Incubator.
- Tianjin Tanggu Marine Technology Incubator.

6.8 Emerging Multinationals

Newly emerging multinational companies are pioneering the drive for China to move up the economic value chain and there are already some success stories.

For example, the Haier Group, a large Chinese household appliance manufacturer which already sells some 10 million refrigerators in global markets, has shifted their focus to the high-end refrigerator market. Haier is spending close to $1 billion on research and innovation to support this high-end product strategy. This level of R&D represents some 6.2% of their global revenues, which is well in excess of their competitors' such as Whirlpool and Electrolux. Furthermore, Haier has nine R&D facilities and 15 information centres in overseas countries and is therefore already operating as a multinational company. In addition, they are now able to initially launch these new high-technology products in the Chinese domestic market where the demand for high-end products has grown rapidly in recent years. They are predicting growth rates of 50% annually for the next few years for these high-end products in international markets.

Other successful, emerging Chinese multinationals include Lenovo (computers), Huawei (telecommunications) and China International Marine Containers, CIMC (containers).

Lenovo is now globally recognized following the historic purchase of the IBM PC computer business in 2007. The company was a spin-out from a computing institute of the Chinese Academy of Sciences, which still retains a shareholding.

Huawei is a global telecom equipment player that has radically reinvented the industry cost structures and now spends 10% of revenues ($8.5 billion in 2005) on R&D. Their products and solutions are deployed in over 100 countries and serve 31 of the world's top 50 operators, as well as over one billion users worldwide. In May 2007, Symantec, the large US-based IT security software company and Huawei announced that the two companies have formed a joint venture company which will develop and distribute security and storage appliances to global telecommunications carriers and enterprises. This represents a formidable global partnership to offer solutions in the telecom equipment and software market.

CIMC has moved from being a low-end, high-volume producer to become the dominant force in world shipping containers with some 55% of the global market. This Chinese multinational has systematically captured the high end of the market including sophisticated refrigeration and electronic tracking systems from high-cost European specialist manufacturers.

6.9 Pharmaceutical Growth

Multinational pharmaceutical companies are faced with ever increasing costs (currently close to $1 billion per new drug) and long lead times (up to 10 years) to develop and bring new products to market. An increasing number of pharmaceutical companies such as Novo Nordisk, Eli Lilly, Pfizer and Astra Zeneca have established research facilities in China to take advantage of lower costs, skilled labour and a large local market.

China is also in the very early stages of building a world-class pharmaceutical industry. The competitive advantages include: substantially lower clinical trial costs (10–20% of those in developed countries), a large population from which to recruit clinical trial patients, a rapidly growing skill pool of biotechnology and medical specialists to manage clinical trials, low-cost drug manufacturing facilities and a very large and growing local market for pharmaceutical products. A new breed of Chinese companies in the health sector is building multinational companies that cover the full pharmaceutical value chain covering drug discovery, clinical trials, Good Manufacturing Practice (GMP) facilities and product marketing.

These new pharmaceutical companies have the potential to dramatically reduce (by 15–25%) the overall costs and (40–60%) time to market for the development of new drugs. These savings of cost and time are so compelling that rapid growth is anticipated for the pharmaceutical industry in China during the next decade. Concerns regarding safety and quality of drug development are already reduced as the Chinese government pharmaceutical regulator (SFDA) continues to introduce clinical trial protocols and manufacturing requirements that meet international standards.

An example of such a Chinese company is Venturepharma, that started out as a healthcare contract research organization and through the recent acquisition of Commonwealth Biotech, based in the US, and with subsidiaries in the UK and Australia, has become a multinational player with the full value chain of pharmaceutical activities. Other emerging pharmaceutical challengers that also offer the full spectrum of the pharmaceutical value chain include WuXi Pharma Tech and ShangPharma.

6.10 Low-Cost Innovation

New business model innovations are now bubbling up from developing economies such as China and India, to threaten the established global giants. In a report from the consultancy, Deloitte, it is argued that the activity of private entrepreneurs means that "China is rapidly emerging as the global centre of management innovation, pioneering management techniques that most US companies are struggling to understand."

These new business models are based on "low-cost and open innovation" in partnership with local suppliers successfully delivering substantial cost reductions, as well as on quality improvements. This low-cost innovation business model is highly disruptive and poses a serious competitive threat to multinational companies that have operations which are still largely concentrated in high-cost developed countries. The current strategy of many multinationals to shift to more advanced and higher added value products to protect their operating margins is unlikely to succeed as new competitors are also moving rapidly into the high-technology end of the global market.

A more successful, though challenging, strategy is to enter the Chinese market and, possibly with local partners, take up the challenge of competing directly with these new multinationals in their home market. To succeed in China, multinational companies will also have to embrace the low-cost innovation model and thereby produce new products and services that will remain competitive in global markets.

Interestingly, many innovative global IT companies such as Google, Microsoft, Sun Microsystems, Adobe Systems, Proctor & Gamble, NEC, Symantec, Toyota, Schlumberger and Fairchild Semiconductor have all set up research facilities in the Tsinghua University Science Park in Beijing as shown in Fig. 6.4.

Fig. 6.4 Tsinghua University Science Park (Author's photo)

This Beijing-based science park provides these multinationals with a "window into China" and access to top-tier Chinese talent from Tsinghua University which is considered to be the "MIT of China". Google, for example, has recently announced a major collaborative project focused on "cloud computing" with Tsinghua University, where there is a strong skill pool in the field of massive parallel computing.

Intel, the world's leading microprocessor maker, has been active in China for some 20 years and has invested more than $1.3 billion in R&D, testing and assembly facilities while growing its sales and marketing operations to cover more than 300 cities. Between 2000 and 2005, the proportion of Intel's revenue in the United States fell from $12.4 billion to $5.7 billion, while those from China rose from $2.1 billion in 2003 to over $5.3 billion in 2005.

Hence a more complex low cost innovation model is now emerging, whereby both Chinese and foreign multinationals are now competing within China for highly skilled labour as shown in Fig. 6.5.

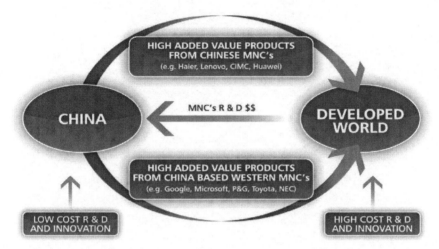

Fig. 6.5 The disruptive Chinese low cost innovation business model (Author's drawing)

In fact, China could very well derive significant synergy from the presence of the foreign multinationals who will impart western innovation management concepts to their local Chinese organizations which will eventually diffuse through into the broader Chinese business community.

As this model gains momentum, low-cost innovation is likely to lead to a new export wave of high-technology products emerging from China, but developed by both Chinese and foreign multinationals. This business model poses a serious competitive threat to western companies that are, either by choice or otherwise, not engaged with this low-cost innovation mega trend.

Over the past few decades, China has successfully built a strong science and technology foundation and is now progressing towards building an innovation infrastructure. This will likely present China with some significant challenges to create both the cultural environment and human resource talent pool that is required to enable innovation to flourish.

Chapter 7
Innovative India

India has a rich history of science and innovation which include discovering the decimal system, advanced geometry and the smelting of iron with carbon to make steel. However, only relatively recently has the Indian economy been open for global business and the result has been an economic transformation with an average GDP growth rate of 8% per annum since 2003.

The rapid economic growth in India can be largely attributed to software development and IT services which were made possible through the rapid rise of the global Internet. In fact, given the poor general infrastructure and high levels of government bureaucracy, it could be argued that without the global adoption of this borderless digital technology, India might still be a large under-developed country.

Further, India is no longer a "command" economy but one driven increasingly by entrepreneurship. The telecommunications infrastructure has made enormous strides, with Internet and mobile phones available even in the remotest villages. India also has huge human resource potential with some 50% of the population (550 million people) being under the age of 24.

Presently, the country has two principal advantages; being the quality of its manpower and a relatively low cost structure whereby numerous products can be manufactured at much lower cost than in most other parts of the world.

7.1 Indian Science and Technology

In India, unlike developed countries, universities tend to be focused only on education and teaching, and research activities are largely carried out in government institutes and company laboratories. The pool of young Indian university graduates is estimated to be 14 million which is twice that of the US. Further, this pool is being topped up by some 2.5 million new graduates in IT, engineering and life sciences each year. However, despite this large and growing pool of talent, the shortage of skilled workers is considered to be the main constraint on Indian innovation.

There are around 38 research institutes that are part of the Council for Scientific and Industrial Research (CSIR). The top-tier institutes within the CSIR system are

I.E. Maxwell, *Managing Sustainable Innovation*,
DOI 10.1007/978-0-387-87581-1_7, © 2009 by Ian E. Maxwell

the National Chemical Laboratory, the Centre for Cellular and Molecular Biology and the Institute of Chemical Technology.

The country also has seven Indian Institutes of Technology (IITs) which are considered to have played a key role in educating the technologists that have driven the growth engine of the Indian economy. However, these IITs are not prolific centres of research.

The Indian Institute of Science, Bangalore, was founded in 1909 by the visionary industrialist, J N Tata. This institute, which has both teaching and research roles, is ranked as the most prestigious university in India and is among the top 60 Asia Pacific universities.

As a catalyst for innovation, a new set of institutions have been designed called the Indian Institutes of Scientific Education and Research (IISERs). These new institutes will include both teaching and research with aspirations to create organizational structures that will have no silos and foster interdisciplinary cross-fertilization. The intention is also to provide teaching at the graduate and post-graduate level in science and technology including the application to business. Pune and Kolkata will be the locations for the first of the IISERs and these new institutions should further enhance the innovation capabilities of India.

7.2 The Indian Disruptive "Low Cost Innovation" Threat

The low-cost innovation model emerging from large, rapidly developing economies such as India and China poses a major threat to the established global multinationals. These new emerging multinationals from India and China are driving forward with a disruptive business model based on both "low cost and open innovation", often in partnership with local suppliers.

As a response to these emerging multinationals, foreign companies are setting up their own R&D facilities and innovation centres in these developing countries as shown in Fig. 7.1.

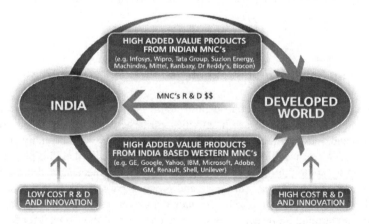

Fig. 7.1 The disruptive Indian low cost innovation business model (Author's drawing)

7.3 Indian Multinationals

Indian companies have, in the past, been overly protected by their government from external competition. However, the new, more open governmental economic policy has enabled Indian companies to become multinationals at impressive speed, ramping up exports, making cross-border corporate alliances and even acquisitions in the US, Europe, and emerging markets.

The large IT-services companies such as Wipro, Infosys Technologies, and Tata Consultancy Services have evolved from outsourcing niche players to multinationals with operations in most major markets. These new global IT giants have created campus-type R&D facilities in India such as those of Infosys to attract and retain top talent.

The Tata group, which is one the largest Indian multinational companies, has recently attracted considerable global attention with the launch of the world's cheapest car. The Tata Nano car is a reflection of emerging innovative India and provides an excellent example of the disruptive low-cost innovation model. In 2003, when Ratan Tata, the 70-year old head of the giant Tata group, revealed plans to build a car that would cost 100,000 rupees ($2,500), his rivals in the global automobile industry were highly sceptical. The global car industry was clearly shaken when the Nano car, as shown in Fig. 7.2, was unveiled in January 2008.

Fig. 7.2 The Tata Nano car (Source: Wikipedia Common)

The Tata Nano car encompasses a great deal of design innovation much of which has been protected with 34 patents. The Nano is much lighter than comparable models as a result of the use of lightweight steel, plastics and an aluminium engine. The car currently meets all Indian emission, pollution and safety standards. Although it only attains a maximum speed of about 65 mph, the fuel efficiency is very high at 50 miles to the gallon. This accomplishment by Tata has led to a flurry of announcements from other car manufacturers who are also now planning to develop smaller, less costly and energy-efficient cars illustrating the global potential of this low-cost innovation megatrend.

At the other end of the automobile spectrum, Tata Motors has exerted its global prowess by purchasing Jaguar and Land Rover. These two grand old names of British car manufacturing will likely be produced in Pune instead of Coventry in the future.

Suzlon which started as an Indian textile manufacturer is now one of the world's leading makers of wind turbines. As part of the strategy to build a global base, Suzlon has made foreign acquisitions which includes Hansen from Belgium and Repower from Germany.

India, long the home of low-cost generic drug manufacturing production, has shown in recent years that they can also achieve the highest technical and ethical standards, develop true innovation and increasingly serve the real health needs of their populations. Many Indian pharmaceutical companies that have grown rapidly in the past decade through low-cost manufacturing of generic drugs are now eager to move up the innovation value chain and develop their own drugs to market both locally and globally. Ranbaxy Laboratories is India's leading pharmaceutical company with both drug development and manufacturing operations. Their drug development focus is in the areas of gastrointestinal, cardiovascular, central nervous system disorders, diabetes, pain, allergies, and HIV/AIDS. In addition, the company also has a groundbreaking anti-malarial drug candidate in late-phase trials.

Dr Reddy's has also grown from a generic drug manufacturer to become a fully integrated pharmaceutical company with a global reach. This path has been accelerated through both collaborations and acquisitions of foreign companies. For example, Dr Reddy's has a joint development program with Rheoscience in Denmark to develop and commercialize a type-2 diabetes drug. In 2004, Reddy's acquired Trigenesis Therapeutics, a US-based private dermatology company, and in 2005, they purchased Betapharm, a large German generics manufacturer with a portfolio of some 150 active pharmaceutical ingredients.

Established in 1978, Biocon is India's leading biotechnology enterprise focused on the development of biopharmaceuticals for diabetes, cardiology and oncology. The company serves partners and customers in over 50 countries and ranks first in Asia in terms of revenues and market capitalization. The company is headed by Kiran Mazumdar-Shaw, India's second richest woman, who achieved this status after Biocon gained a market capitalization of $1 billion on the first day of listing on the Indian stock exchange in 2004.

7.4 Foreign R&D Centres

India has gained in the globalization of R&D and now ranks sixth in the world as a destination for establishing such innovation centres as shown in Fig. 7.3.

General Motors (GM), for example, has recently opened a new design centre based in Bangalore incorporating virtual reality technology. This facility is intended to be fully incorporated into the 11 design centres that are part of the GM global network.

Fig. 7.3 The globalization of R&D (redrawn from source)

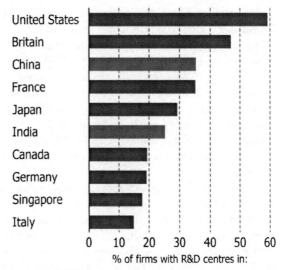

% of firms with R&D centres in:

Source:UNCTAD survey of big R&D spenders

Google chose Bangalore in 2004 as the site of its first R&D centre outside the US, partly since many Googlers, who were of Indian extraction, wanted to move back to India and participate in the country's new found growth. Google's experiment in replicating its Silicon Valley workplace indulgences in Bangalore and luring back the Indian talent that helped fuel the dot-com boom in the US was a deliberate strategy effectively creating a brain drain in reverse (Fig. 7.4).

Fig. 7.4 The Googleplex in Bangalore (Source: Copyright Google)

Interestingly, Google Bangalore has a wide range of diversity with Sikhs, Hindus, Muslims, Buddhists and Christians as part of the talent pool. Being highly educated, they speak English, but they also speak Hindi, Tamil, Bengali, Telugu and several more of India's 22 officially recognized languages.

The John F. Welch Technology Centre, opened in Bangalore in 2000, is a multi-disciplinary research and development centre that collaborates with three other R&D facilities in Schenectady, Munich and Shanghai to conduct research development and engineering activities for all of GE's diverse businesses worldwide. The Bangalore facility has leading-edge facilities for research and development in such diverse fields from mechanical and electrical engineering to polymer science and chemical engineering.

The Shell Group has also recently opened a research & development facility in Bangalore and plan to expand to 1000 professionals in the near future. This new technical centre offers high-end technical careers in a global environment to both local and experienced Indian professionals from around the world who see India as their base. The Anglo-Dutch consumer product giant, Unilever, also has a research facility in Bangalore as part of a global network of six R&D centres in the UK, Netherlands, US and China.

India now needs to move to the next phase of economic development by moving up the innovation value chain and create new products rather than simply providing IT and pharmaceutical services. This will require further investment in the existing science and technology foundation as well as building both a strong innovation and physical infrastructure. The current endemic government bureaucracy will also need to be streamlined. If these challenges can be overcome, India could potentially create a high-growth, low-cost and sustainable innovation driven economy.

Chapter 8
Innovative Tigers

In recent years, many countries around the world have recognized that innovation is vital for sustainable economic growth. Under the influence of global economic forces, many developed countries are driving innovation in an attempt to create higher added value products and services to compensate for their higher cost structures. At the same time, large developing economies such as China and India are also stimulating innovation in order to move up this value chain. In this manner, they are targeting the achievement of higher margins through greater ownership of the intellectual property created for new products and services delivered to both local and global markets.

The following countries have been selected to provide examples where interesting approaches to building an innovation infrastructure are already achieving some success, although this may not yet be apparent in the country innovation rankings.

8.1 Singapore Biotech Gamble

The Singapore government has achieved remarkable results in terms of raising the GDP per capita of the country to the top quartile of the OECD and the 7th place in the GII innovation ranking (see Chapter 1) within a decade. This has been achieved by moving the economy from a largely manufacturing base to a more modern regime in which high technology plays a much stronger role. Foreign companies have been provided with financial incentives to set up R&D facilities in Singapore and the government has invested heavily to create a strong, supporting innovation infrastructure.

As a small country, the Singapore government has decided to focus this investment primarily in the area of biotechnology aiming to become the biomedical hub of Asia. The creation of the billion-dollar Biopolis biomedical science and technology park has been a cornerstone investment to develop the necessary infrastructure.

The Singapore Economic Development Board (EDB) plays a key role in developing and implementing the government economic vision. Interestingly, the EDB has a venture capital group who not only provide early stage co-funding for local companies but also invest globally in areas of technology that could become important for Singapore in the future. For example, the EDB was a highly valued, early-stage

I.E. Maxwell, *Managing Sustainable Innovation*,
DOI 10.1007/978-0-387-87581-1_8, © 2009 by Ian E. Maxwell

investor in the high throughput process company, Avantium, based in the Netherlands, in which the author was a co-founder.

However, in order to remain competitive in the new global knowledge economy, Singapore may also need to seek partnerships in biotechnology with emerging low-cost innovation countries such as India and China. In this regard, the government plan to increase immigration from these countries would fit well with such an innovation integration strategy.

Another challenge for Singapore could be the fact that, while the biotechnology sector has historically required high levels of investment into research and technology, it has, to date, not provided strong financial rewards. There are only a handful of biotech companies in the world such as Amgen and Genentech which have prospered and are both profitable and generating strong revenue growth.

8.2 Israel High-Tech Exports

Israel provides another example of a small, developed country that has proactively developed a powerful innovation infrastructure and thereby created a strong knowledge-based sector of its economy. Remarkably, high-technology exports accounted for some 46% of total exports in 2007, moving the country from a past deficit to a balance of payments surplus. This export growth has been supported by the technology sector of the Israeli economy which has been expanding at the rate of 10–20% over the past 5 years.

Israel has also invested heavily in building a strong innovation infrastructure with science parks being a primary component. In addition, the government has successfully attracted global technology giants such as Microsoft, Intel, Motorola and IBM to establish local R&D centres in Israel. Interestingly, Israel has an R&D spend of 4.4% per capita, which achieves the top ranking in the world.

However, although Israel is a prolific spawning ground for high-tech start-up companies, many of them are acquired by foreign companies and effectively exported. At present, therefore, Israel finds itself positioned at the front end of the innovation value chain which, in the long term, will likely not provide the highest economic added value.

More recently, Israel has attracted attention from the clean fuels global community with Project Better Place, the brainchild of an entrepreneur, called Shai Agassi. This project involves the development of a rechargeable grid system in Israel for electric cars. The company has raised around $200 million from Israeli and US venture capital companies and plans to build 500,000 charging points by 2011. Renault-Nissan, who has announced ambitious plans for plug-in cars, will supply the electric vehicles for the project. Interestingly, the infrastructure will be largely supplied by solar-generated electric power making this a practically zero-emissions project. This could potentially enable Israel to become a leader in electric vehicle infrastructure and thereby create a major global business opportunity, much as Denmark has become a world leader in wind power.

8.3 The United Arab Emirates Renewable Future

The United Arab Emirates (UAE) has ambitious goals to broaden its economic base beyond the current high dependence on the production and export of crude oil. As part of a long-term plan to build the necessary educational infrastructure, the Dubai Knowledge Village (DKV) was launched in 2003 with the goal of becoming the Middle East destination for learning excellence as shown in Fig. 8.1.

Fig. 8.1 The Dubai Knowledge Village (Source: Wikimedia Commons)

This new knowledge community was founded as part of a long-term economic strategy to develop the region's talent pool and accelerate its move into a knowledge-based economy.

An even more ambitious UAE megaproject is the creation of a sustainable, zero-carbon, zero-waste city called Masdar in the Abu Dhabi emirate at a projected cost of $22 billion. This novel six square kilometre city, which will become the home to 50,000 people and 1,500 businesses, will rely entirely on solar energy and other renewable energy sources such as wind and geothermal. The first phase of the city construction is expected to be completed by 2009.

A further initiative is the founding of a new university called the Masdar Institute of Science and Technology (MIST), which will be established in partnership with the Massachusetts Institute of Technology (MIT) in the US. The research at this new institute will focus on renewable energy and a $250 million Clean Technology fund has also been established to support start-up companies emerging from the university research partnership. This well-developed strategy is clearly aimed at creating an innovation hub for renewable energy in the UAE.

A major challenge for the UAE and other Middle East countries will be to build a strong enough science and technology foundation to support the developing innovation infrastructure. Highly skilled human resources and the creation of an innovative culture will all be crucial elements for success in addition to massive levels of financial investment.

8.4 Finland Beyond Mobile Phones

Finland provides an inspiring story of a small, developed country of only 5 million people who, over the past 15 years, has been able to reinvent an economy that in the early 1990s was on the brink of disaster. The stellar rise of the mobile phone giant Nokia, from a slow-moving conglomerate to a global technology powerhouse, is quite remarkable. This economic transformation has been achieved by building a strong scientific and educational foundation and then creating an innovative infrastructure and culture to enable a knowledge-intensive economy to flourish.

Finland became the first country in the world to introduce the concept of a national innovation system in which networking and cooperation became the norm for both public-private partnerships and governance of the country. This innovation-driven economic transformation lifted the GDP per capita of the country to the current ranking level of 18th position in the world.

However, Nokia remains dominant in Finnish business, contributing some 20% of manufacturing exports and 40% of the industrial R&D spend. Further, the rapid growth in costs and wages make Finland vulnerable to competition from low-cost innovation countries that are increasingly benefiting from the globalization of technology and knowledge. Moreover, the recent entry of new and powerful players such as Google with their Android software and Apple with the iPhone into the global mobile phone market poses a threat to the dominant position of Nokia.

All of these developments mean that Finland will be challenged to drive their innovation machine harder to ensure that they continue to develop exciting new products and services in the telecommunications and IT sectors where they have built such a strong technological base.

8.5 New Zealand Needs to be Bold

The New Zealand (NZ) economy is still dominated by the export of primary produce such as meat and dairy products and tourism. More recently, there has been a drive by the government to broaden this relatively narrow base and move towards a more knowledge-oriented economy.

A number of measures have been taken to build an innovation infrastructure such as introducing a research and development (R&D) tax credit for all qualifying businesses and even non-profit organizations. The tax credit is advantageous to early-stage high technology companies that are not yet paying tax as they receive a cash payment through this scheme. In fact, some 20 countries in the OECD have now introduced some form of R&D tax benefit. This mechanism of stimulating innovation has a significant advantage over direct grants in that, market forces, rather than government departments, determine the selection and direction of R&D programmes.

Another interesting initiative has been to create a government-backed venture fund to co-invest, with early-stage venture capital, to projects that are perceived to offer high growth for the NZ economy. This effectively reduces the risk for venture capital companies and acts as a stimulus for this crucial element of the country's innovation structure. Since the venture capital industry in NZ is at an early stage of development, this is another useful tool to accelerate innovation.

For developed countries with small but highly educated populations such as NZ, the most effective stimulation model is likely to be one that is focused on the early part of the innovation value chain. Globalization of technology can then be achieved through smart integration of new developments with other parts of the value chain.

For example, Right Hemisphere is a company that was created and initially supported by early-stage venture capital in NZ. The company has developed novel software to enable the multiple formats of 3D computer-aided design (CAD) of complex products to be integrated into a single format to support, for example, marketing, training, maintenance and service of these products. Once the concept related to this technology was proven in NZ, the company was able to attract major funding from Silicon Valley venture capital companies such as Sequoia and Sutter Hill to further develop the technology and, perhaps more importantly, secure business with major global companies in the aerospace, defence, automotive and energy industries such as General Dynamics, Pratt & Whitney, Sikorsky, Airbus, Daimler Chrysler and Siemens.

As shown in Fig. 8.2, the software can be used to create single format 3D images of highly complex products such as jet aircraft.

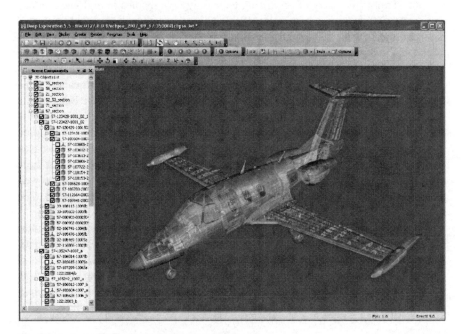

Fig. 8.2 A single 3D format image of a jet aircraft
(Source: Courtesy of Eclipse Aviation Corporation, 2008)

This 3D image can then be used, for example, to enable fast and efficient training of maintenance engineers to provide service support for this product all over the world. Right Hemisphere has since set up large marketing, sales and customer support teams in the US while retaining the cutting-edge research and development in NZ. The company is now moving towards a more sustainable innovation model in which the quantum innovation will be carried out at its central research facilities in NZ and the incremental innovations at development sites in the US, Europe and Asia in closer proximity to its customers. In order to spawn new applications of this powerful 3D software platform, the NZ government has funded the formation of a new non-profit company called NextSpace to act as a propagation vehicle.

Another innovative NZ company, Netvalue, has developed a powerful algorithm called SLIM search, which is highly efficient for searching very large data bases in the multi-terabyte range. This development is very timely with new DNA machines sequencing billions of base pairs and generating terabytes of data. Advanced search technology is vital to be able to correlate these massive base pair sequences with important gene-related effects such as predicting individual human response to therapeutic drugs and the propensity for developing particular diseases. The power of SLIM search was recently demonstrated, whereby the software tool was capable of determining the relationships between the genomes of some 600 bacteria, totalling 2.2 billion base pairs, in minutes on a single PC and, in just seconds on a cluster of computers, representing a quantum innovation in search technology.

The NZ government has implemented so-called "beachhead programmes" to actively support the entry of promising technology companies into global markets and thereby stimulate the integration of the innovation value chain. In addition, NZ has been the first OECD country to sign a free trade agreement with China. It is hoped that this will lead to cooperation in technology areas showing synergism and hence to partnerships in innovation to the benefit of both countries.

However, the persistent, low added-value bias of the economy has meant that the country has experienced a steady decline in the OECD ranking of GDP per capita over the past two decades. The NZ government's target to return to the upper quartile ranking can only be achieved if measures are taken to further boost the innovation infrastructure and provide a strong stimulus to rapidly grow the knowledge-based sector of the economy. Given the historical strength in primary products, the bold move for NZ might be to invest heavily into animal and plant genomics to be well positioned for the impending wave of gene technology innovation that appears to be imminent.

These are some examples of developed and developing countries that are becoming a new breed of innovative tigers who are striving to build a sustainable innovation infrastructure and compete in the global economy. Countries that do not embrace this innovation megatrend will likely struggle to raise living standards in the new knowledge-based economy and risk becoming marginalized in the future.

Chapter 9
Big Bets Innovation

Large, publicly listed multinational companies are under intense pressure from shareholders to deliver both high and sustainable growth rates or suffer severe penalties, as reflected in their global stock market prices. Since the revenue bases of these organizations are already in the multi-billion dollar range, this often means that these conglomerates need to make some "big bets" in their research, technology development and innovation pipeline in order to achieve the growth rates demanded by their shareholders.

Industries that are faced with "big bet" innovation challenges include well-established business sectors such as pharmaceuticals, energy, IT, telecommunications, aerospace, car manufacturing, bulk chemicals and power generation. Some of these innovation "big bets" have paid off handsomely and others have resulted in major write-offs. It is instructive to review some notable recent successes and failures.

9.1 Big Oil Bets

The giant multinational energy company, Shell, is a good example of a company that has taken many "big bets" with a track record of numerous big successes and, inevitably, a few big failures.

These "big bets" over the past few decades have included the development of deep water drilling and production technology, coal gasification technology, gas to liquids technology (GTL), shale oil recovery and processing, and the discovery, development and marketing of a novel polymeric material. The time lines for these mega projects are of the order of one to three decades and cumulative costs in the billion dollar range.

Shell recognized some decades ago that, while global oil reserves were depleting rapidly, there were still large untapped reserves of natural gas. However, a significant amount of this natural gas is located in remote areas and cannot be easily brought to large consumer markets. Shell, therefore, embarked on a major project to convert natural gas (largely methane) into more valuable liquid hydrocarbons that could be more easily transported. The GTL technology involves the conversion of

I.E. Maxwell, *Managing Sustainable Innovation*,
DOI 10.1007/978-0-387-87581-1_9, © 2009 by Ian E. Maxwell

methane into so-called synthesis gas (a mixture of carbon monoxide and hydrogen) and the conversion of this gas mixture into mainly liquid hydrocarbons that can be used as high quality fuels and primarily "clean" diesel. These processes involve the use of sophisticated catalyst systems that greatly enhance the efficiency of the overall system and have been developed and further refined over many years of intensive research at the Shell laboratories in Amsterdam.

The first GTL commercial plant based on Shell technology was constructed in Bintulu in Malaysia and has been successfully in operation since 1993. A second, very large plant is now under construction in Qatar called Pearl GTL and will be operational in 2010. Other companies such as Sasol and Chevron have also developed similar technology and are building plants in Qatar and Nigeria. These new "synthetic" fuels produced from GTL technology are environmentally very "clean" as they are free of sulphur and aromatic compounds, and now offer an economically viable, alternative route to produce high quality transportation fuel alongside the refining of crude oil.

Shell was also early to recognize the huge untapped potential of tar sands as a rich source of hydrocarbons and started research as far back as 1981 to explore how to develop technology to economically extract these valuable hydrocarbons embedded in shale rock deposits mainly in Alberta in Canada. The oil giant not only invested in the extraction technology but also developed modified hydro-processing technology to upgrade this so-called syncrude oil to produce high quality transportation fuels. A Shell refinery in Edmonton, for example, has been specifically designed to efficiently process this valuable syncrude and thus provided Canada with very large indigenous source of fossil fuels.

Deep water drilling is another area in which a number of large energy companies have invested heavily in new technologies to extend oil and gas exploration. Working in such difficult locations requires companies to overcome a number of tough technical challenges. These include finding new ways to build vast floating factories that can venture into ever-greater depths, designing new equipment to work in the intense cold and crushing pressure of water thousands of metres deep and finding profitable ways to tap reservoirs scattered across many miles. These deep water projects have become increasingly ambitious pushing into waters 3,000 metres (about 9,800 ft) deep and more.

New world records for the depth of offshore projects continue to be set on a regular basis as energy companies explore ever further into this hostile environment, driven by the need to find and extract scarcer fossil fuel resources. The push into the deep is likely to accelerate, since most of today's deep water projects are expected to peak by about 2012. This will drive a second and third wave of exploration into more remote and fragmented reservoirs and stimulate technological innovation to make it possible.

The dark depths of today's deep water projects, which are among the lowest points on the planet explored by man, present another set of crucial challenges. In these pitch-dark surroundings, robotic submarines, operated remotely from the surface, are indispensable. About the size of a car, they carry lights and cameras, sharing the icy environment with rarely seen species of fish while conducting the intricate work of installing the complex infrastructure of wells, pumps and pipes on the sea floor. The weight of thousands of metres of water bearing down exerts extreme pressure on equipment which is almost 350 times the average air pressure at sea level.

To withstand these enormous deep water pressures, Shell and others are adopting carbon fibre and other strong, lightweight composite materials already used in the aerospace industry. These new, lighter materials, needed for the next generation of projects in ultra-deep water, are likely to be deployed around the turn of the present decade.

Under the combination of near-freezing temperatures and high pressures on the seabed, oil tends to congeal. Gas and water mingled with oil form ice-like hydrates which can block pipes. Companies solve this problem by adding chemicals to prevent freezing and, more recently, Shell has taken inspiration from marine life to develop new synthetic chemicals based on fish protein to do the job better and more cheaply.

Another focus of deep water oil and gas research is to place as much equipment on the sea floor as possible to reduce or eliminate the need for production platforms. For example, at Ormen Lange, a joint project in which Shell is a partner to develop a gas field off the Norwegian coast, project engineers are investigating ways to install compressors on the sea floor to provide the pressure necessary to transport the gas to shore. If successful, that would eliminate the need to use an offshore platform that will otherwise be required when the natural pressure in the field tails off in several years. Such subsea projects will become increasingly attractive as oil prices continue to rise. The Norwegian energy giant, Statoil, recently installed the world's first commercial subsea processing unit at their Tordis field in the North Sea.

Cost-effective subsea systems to accelerate production and boost reserves will become crucial in the development of offshore deepwater fields in remote or harsh environments. Subsea systems may also hold the answer to the difficult environmental and geopolitical questions posed by the resources hidden beneath the Arctic. It has been estimated that up to 25% of the world's undiscovered reserves are in Arctic areas. With no above-water elements, oil and gas could be recovered from under the ice or in key fishing grounds and produced direct to shore. This innovative technology could provide a solution to many of the environmental issues often associated with oil and gas production in such sensitive areas.

9.2 Big Chemical Bets

Not all big bets have been successful. The chemicals arm of Shell took a "big bet" to develop, manufacture and market a new polymer based on a discovery by one of their most creative researchers, Eite Drent, at the Shell laboratories in Amsterdam in the early 1990s. The invention involved the serendipitous discovery of a novel catalyst system that enabled carbon monoxide and ethylene to be combined to form a new polymeric material called "polyketone" and later given the commercial trade name of Carilon. The new polymer was shown to have some very attractive thermoplastic properties with potential applications in the automobile, electronics, consumer appliances and textile industries.

Some 13 years later, after spending close to $1 billion on process research and development, pilot plant testing, full scale manufacturing facilities, product development and marketing, the company pulled the plug on the project. In hindsight, this innovation challenge proved to be just "too big" for a bulk chemical company that had only very limited previous experience in taking a totally new polymer to market. Fortunately, the integration of Shell Chemicals with the Shell Group's highly profitable oil and gas business enabled them to recover from such a major financial write-off.

The lesson offered from this example is that companies should be continuously self-critical of their core competencies along the innovation value chain and not hesitate to seek partners to fill their own skill and experience gaps and in this way "speed to market" can be improved and costly errors avoided. In 2002, Shell donated the extensive Carilon patent portfolio to SRI International, a leading non-profit research institute based in Silicon Valley, California.

Interestingly, as the oil majors are now confronted with the challenge of a significant shift towards renewable energy, they appear to be recognizing their competency gaps and are forming partnerships, often with young companies, to gain access to new skills and rapidly emerging technologies. For example, Shell recently announced a joint venture called Avancis with Saint-Gobain Glass to begin solar power panel manufacturing based on advanced thin-film, cadmium-indium-selenide (CIS) technology. Shell has formed another joint venture with a Hawaiian-based start-up company that is developing biofuels from algae. The British energy giant, BP, appears to be even more adventurous and is backing Synthetic Genomics to develop a synthetic microbe that is capable of converting coal into methane gas.

9.3 Big Pharma Bets

Pfizer also took a "Big Bet" when it attempted to pair its highly successful drug, Lipitor, which reduces low density (LDL) "bad" cholesterol in the body with a novel drug, Torcetrapib, which has the effect of increasing high density (HDL) "good" cholesterol. HDL was known to clear plaques from arteries and hence should reduce the risk of heart attacks. Unfortunately, disaster struck in the final phase of human trials when a number of patients died of heart attacks. The drug development of Torcetrapib was immediately terminated and the share price of Pfizer slumped 10% on the stock market.

It has now been discovered that Torcetrapib induced toxicity by turning up the production of a chemical called aldosterone which increased blood pressure and resulted in fatal heart attacks. The research and development including clinical trials on Torcetrapib cost Pfizer $1 billion and they were left without a replacement drug for the blockbuster Lipitor that will soon come off-patent and plummet in price.

Another pharmaceutical giant, Merck, has also recently suffered a severe setback with a blockbuster drug called Vioxx. This non-steroidal anti-inflammatory drug was used to treat osteoarthritis and acute pain conditions but was pulled from the market in 2004 after it was linked to the risk of strokes and heart attacks. Vioxx was one of the most widely used drugs ever to be withdrawn from the market. In the year before withdrawal, Merck had sales revenue of $2.5 billion from this drug.

Not only has Merck lost a major source of revenue from this drug but has also faced numerous lawsuits in the past few years. A settlement of $4.9 billion has recently been reached for 27,000 lawsuits which, it is hoped, will end this chapter of litigation for Merck and substantially reduce companies' legal fees currently amounting to $600 million per annum.

A mechanism proposed to explain the heart attacks caused by Vioxx involved the suppression of a molecule called prostaglandin, an anti-clotting agent in the blood. Perhaps the lesson for Pfizer, Merck and, possibly, other pharmaceutical companies is that research on the basic biological chemistry should go hand-in-hand with drug discovery and clinical trials. A deeper understanding of the fundamental biochemistry of these drug molecules might have avoided these massive costs at the final phase of the innovation value chain. Furthermore, it might prove cost effective to outsource this more fundamental supporting biochemical research to university or contract research organizations under strict confidentiality.

It is fortunate that, in general, these big pharmaceutical companies have other highly profitable drugs in the market and alternative new drugs in their research and development pipelines to absorb these massive losses. While these large companies often receive quite negative publicity, they have developed highly sophisticated innovation engines and the financial resources to take "big bets" to develop new and highly effective drugs to improve global human health.

9.4 Big Car Bets

Toyota placed a "big bet" almost a decade ago when they developed and produced the first hybrid petrol and electric vehicle, called the Prius. This innovation was viewed by many of the large global automobile companies as an expensive and risky venture into a small, niche market. To date, Toyota has sold more than a million of these hybrids and has recently announced plans to develop hybrid power trains for all their models. This technology lead in hybrid vehicles, has placed Toyota in a strong competitive position as the industry moves further towards the all-electric plug-in vehicle.

In contrast, a number of the large US automobile manufacturers such as General Motors (GM) and Ford, who have resisted the global trend towards hybrid and electric vehicles, are now strategically disadvantaged compared with their innovative

Japanese rivals such as Toyota and Nissan. The shift to electric vehicles could prove to be an innovation that is highly disruptive towards players in the industry that lack the competencies and technology to make this transition at sufficient speed.

Honda has also made a "big bet" into hydrogen-based fuel cells as a new technology to power motor vehicles with zero emissions. In a fuel cell stack, hydrogen combines catalytically with atmospheric oxygen and the chemical energy from the reaction is converted into electric power which is used to propel the vehicle. After many years of research and development, Honda has recently launched a car based on this technology called the FCX Clarity. This new vehicle is actually a type of hybrid where a hydrogen fuel cell stack is combined with a battery pack. Additional energy is captured through regenerative braking and deceleration and stored in the lithium-ion battery pack to provide supplementary power when required. Honda has developed an innovative Home Energy Station Unit that converts natural gas into hydrogen to provide a possible solution to the refuelling infrastructure issue with the fuel cell. Following a period of intense interest in hydrogen fuel cell technology, it now appears that Honda will struggle to compete with the potential rapid rise of the plug-in electric vehicle.

As new technologies emerge at ever increasing rates, the challenges for large multinational companies in almost every business sector can only become greater; their continued success will require them to pick the right "big bets" to ensure that they are not displaced by quantum or even disruptive innovation from their competitors. This will require a new breed of globally minded and agile management that is able to embrace new concepts such as open innovation and to select mutually beneficial strategic partnerships at all parts of the innovation value chain.

Chapter 10
Renewable Energy Innovation

The compelling evidence of global climate change, the high rate of energy consumption, limited fossil fuel resources and increasing awareness of environmental issues have all contributed to a revitalized interest in renewable energy technologies. Technological innovation will play a major role in tackling these global energy issues which, together with the current rapid diffusion of technologies, will offer high rewards to successful players in this field.

Many of these innovations will likely be incremental, driving down a cost curve for existing renewable technologies, but the huge challenges of reducing carbon dioxide emissions at economically acceptable costs could spawn some disruptive innovation. The global energy market is so huge that renewable energy innovation will be challenged by the gigantic scale of this business sector.

Renewable technology patents have grown significantly in recent years reaching some 900 granted in the US in 2007, as tracked by the so-called Clean Energy Patent Growth Index (CEPGI). Renewable energy is growing rapidly with about 30–40 gigawatts of renewable power installed around the world and $21 billion in global venture capital being invested in new companies in 2007.

A major milestone in climate change has been achieved by the reports from the Intergovernmental Panel on Climate Change (IPCC) which has provided a solid scientific basis for governments to take action. The IPPC together with Al Gore received the 2007 Nobel Peace Prize "for their efforts to build up and disseminate greater knowledge about man-made climate change and to lay the foundations for the measures that are needed to counteract such change".

Progress achieved by the IPCC as well as other key global conferences and follow-on agreements to the Kyoto Protocol, which expires in 2012, will have a major impact on the financial and human resources that will become available for innovation in the renewable technology arena in the near future.

Solar energy is rapidly gaining momentum with the sun-drenched southwestern states in the US legislating minimum solar requirements in their new renewable portfolio standards. Examples include Nevada with 20% by 2015, Arizona with 15% by 2025 and New Mexico with 20% by 2020.

I.E. Maxwell, *Managing Sustainable Innovation*,
DOI 10.1007/978-0-387-87581-1_10, © 2009 by Ian E. Maxwell

10.1 Mediterranean Renewable Energy

The Trans-Mediterranean Renewable Energy Cooperation (TREC) is a highly ambitious plan to create a super grid based on renewable power generation across Europe, North Africa and the Middle East. Renewable power would be generated from a wide variety of sources that would include concentrated solar power (CSP), photovoltaic solar (PV), wind, hydroelectric, wave, biomass and geothermal power. It is estimated that by 2050, somewhere between 10% and 25% of the electricity requirements of Europe could be generated by solar power imported from the sunny deserts of the Middle East and Africa.

Clearly, this massive and highly ambitious project would potentially provide an enormous impulse to renewable energy innovation among the member countries of TREC and dramatically reduce their current reliance on fossil fuels by the year 2050. The major challenge will likely be to achieve the high level of political, technical and commercial cooperation that will be required of all the participant countries to make the project succeed.

10.2 Google RE Less than Coal

To the surprise of many financial commentators, Google has recently announced a new strategic initiative to develop electricity from renewable energy resources that will be cheaper than that produced from coal. The initiative is termed RE$\leq$C (mathematical symbols for "renewable energy equal to or less than coal") and will initially focus on advanced solar and wind power technologies.

Google is not completely new to renewable energy as they have gained quite some expertise by designing and building energy-efficient data centres. Moreover, they deploy solar energy panels on the roof of their headquarters building in Mountain View, California.

The Google goal is to produce one gigawatt (enough to power a city the size of San Francisco) of renewable energy capacity that is cheaper than coal within years, not decades. Since coal currently supplies some 40% of the world's electricity, this is indeed a goal with the potential to significantly reduce carbon emissions.

This new project is being funded through Google.org, the philanthropic arm of the company which invests heavily in R&D projects. The plan is to collaborate with a variety of organizations in the renewable energy field, including companies, research laboratories and universities. Two Californian companies have already been identified as partners that are developing promising scalable technologies. The Google strategy seems to be more focused towards the end of the innovation value chain in line with their ambitious time line to achieve the one gigawatt of renewable power generation.

Some of the partner companies include eSolar Inc, an innovative renewable company that is developing relatively low-cost solar thermal power systems that can be deployed by electricity utility companies. The design is based on modules each generating 25 megawatts (MW) which can be scaled to produce over 500 MW of power. These systems make use of thousands of heliostats as shown in Fig. 10.1 that efficiently concentrate the solar power (CSP) and are mass produced to reduce costs.

Fig. 10.1 A schematic of the eSolar heliostat arrays (Source: Wikimedia commons)

eSolar believe that these renewable power systems will be ideal for energy generation in sun-rich geographies such as the Southwest of the US and, possibly, also the Middle East.

Makani Power, another Google partner, is developing high-altitude wind energy systems that will compete with coal-fired power stations. High-altitude wind energy has the largest energy density per square metre compared to other renewable energy technologies. Although details of the Makani technology have not yet been revealed, they have successfully raised $10 million of series A venture capital funding which also included Google.

The well-defined milestone of the Google initiative should be quite a powerful force to drive renewable energy forward to large scale, commercially viable applications and should, therefore, be warmly welcomed.

10.3 Solar Storage

One of the major disadvantages of solar energy is the intermittent power generation. Another new company, called SolarReserve, backed by United Technologies, aims to construct concentrated solar power (CSP) towers, similar to eSolar, and store the energy in the form of molten salts. The salts consist of a mixture of sodium and potassium nitrate that are melted at the high temperatures from the concentrated solar energy; this latent heat is then released as required through exchangers to produce steam and drive turbines to generate electrical power. Solar-Reserve is planning a large installation that will generate up to 500 MW of power.

10.4 Eco-military

The US military is the single largest energy consumer in the world and it is therefore hardly surprising that, according to the web site Earth2tech, they have recently announced the completion of a 14 MW solar power system based on photovoltaics. This impressive array of 72,000 solar panels, spread over 140 acres in Nevada, as shown in Fig. 10.2, will generate a quarter of the power requirement of the Air Force base and will be the largest photovoltaic system in North America.

The Air Force claims that the project will provide a power saving of about $1 million per year and is considered as a renewable energy test bed for the Department of Defence.

Fig. 10.2 The US Air Force solar panel arrays in Nevada (Source: Wikimedia commons)

10.5 Renewable Venturing

Venture capital companies have been quick to realize these high-growth business opportunities and there has been a major shift towards investment in green technology start-up companies. According to the Clean Edge consulting company, venture capital investment in clean technology will exceed $3 billion for the US. China is expected to become the world's biggest market for clean tech and venture capital already accounts for 20% of Chinese early stage funding. Moreover, DT Capital, based in Shanghai, claim that almost all clean ventures in China are immediately profitable.

Clean Edge research has made the following global market growth projections:

- Biofuels will grow from $20.5 billion in 2006 to $80.9 billion by 2016.
- Wind power is projected to expand from $17.9 billion in 2006 to $60.8 billion in 2016.
- Solar photovoltaics will grow from a $15.6 billion industry in 2006 to $69.3 billion by 2016.
- Fuel cell and distributed hydrogen market will grow from a $1.4 billion industry to $15.6 billion over the next decade.

Altogether, these markets for clean energy technologies are projected to increase from $55 billion in 2006 to reach $226 billion market by 2016. The investment in these green technology start-ups is very different from that of a typical IT company. A high level of investment is required in the research and development phase followed by major funding to build the first commercial manufacturing facility.

10.6 Sky Sails

High fuel costs have driven innovation in the merchant navy with the world's first commercial merchant ship, MV Beluga SkySails, testing a huge kite to catch strong winds up to 300 metres above the surface near Hamburg as shown in Fig. 10.3.

The high-tech kite, the so-called "SkySails" system, reduces fuel consumption and greenhouse gas emissions. This sail system is a giant computer-guided $725,000 kite tethered to the mast and is projected to cut fuel costs by about 20%. The 433-foot long MV "Beluga SkySails" will shortly make its maiden voyage across the Atlantic to Venezuela, up to Boston and then back to Europe.

Fig. 10.3 Skysails system
(Copyright SkySails)

10.7 First Generation Biofuels

Biofuels have attracted a great deal of interest in recent years as a source of renewable energy to reduce the global dependence on fossil fuels. For many countries, this has also been driven by a strategic policy move to become less dependent on imported crude oil. It is noteworthy that the global liquid fuels market is a staggering $3 trillion, which means that the penetration rate of biofuels, even with a strong country governmental support, will be slow and require massive levels of capital investment.

In general, biofuels are either in the form of an additive to gasoline such as ethanol (which should really be termed biogasoline) or plant-derived oils that are added to diesel to produce biodiesel. In each case, the pure plant-derived products can also be used but, in the case of gasoline, the automobile needs to be modified to handle the pure biofuel.

However, there are now growing concerns that biofuels are competing strongly with food production as is evidenced by recent global increases in food cereal costs. For example, the US corn harvest for biofuels has increased from 12 to 16% in the period 2003 to 2006. Moreover, to meet the US government's goal of 35 billion gallons of biofuel per year by 2017, some 40% of the corn harvest will need to be diverted to transportation fuels.

The UN has now become embroiled in the global issue of balancing the development of renewable biofuels against the potential negative impact of rising food prices on global poverty. Second generation biofuel technology offers a potential solution to this growing global dilemma and probably deserves much more financial support for research and development from governments than is currently the case.

10.8 Second Generation Biofuels

Second generation (2G) biofuel development is starting to gain momentum, with technologies targeting to produce products with improved energy density or, more importantly, plant-based products that do not compete with food crops. These 2G biofuel innovations have the potential to become disruptive and displace first generation ethanol technologies. Interestingly, the market conditions for US ethanol producers are already starting to deteriorate due to the rising costs of corn and over production of ethanol.

10.9 Cellulosic Ethanol

Traditional ethanol is produced by fermentation of food-based feedstock such as corn, sugarcane and potatoes, whereas cellulosic ethanol is made from plant fibre such as corn stalks, bagasse from sugarcane processing, straw and potentially woodchips and, therefore, does not compete with food supplies. However, the cellulose is more difficult to convert to ethanol and requires the development of new, efficient cellulose-conversion enzymes.

Iogen, a Canadian company, in partnership with Shell, has developed a process that they claim is economically viable to convert cellulosic biomass into fuel ethanol. The innovative process involves a number of steps which includes a steam pre-treatment, an enzyme hydrolysis step to convert the treated cellulose into glucose, an advanced enzymatic conversion of both C6 and C5 sugars and, finally, a distillation step to purify the ethanol fuel product. This process has apparently been successfully demonstrated in a pilot plant facility in Ottawa yielding some 350 litres of ethanol per tonne of fibre.

Another Canadian company called SunOpta has developed similar technology and has announced plans to jointly build a 10 million gallon per year cellulosic plant with Central Minnesota Ethanol Cooperative (CMEC) in the US. However, possibly, the most advanced biomass project is based in Salamanca in Spain where Abgegoa Bioenergy is nearing the completion of a commercial scale plant to convert agriculture residues such as straw and corn stalks into fuel grade ethanol. This new plant will process some 70 tonnes of cellulosic biomass and produce over 5 million litres of ethanol per year.

These innovative and large scale biomass process developments do appear to open an attractive alternative route to produce fuel from biomass without competing with plant food supplies. However, there is probably still a great deal of scope to further improve the efficiency of the critical enzymatic process steps.

10.10 Beyond Ethanol

Ethanol, which is currently the plant-produced additive used in most biogasoline, has a number of disadvantages such as being less energy efficient and more corrosive than conventional hydrocarbon-based gasoline. To tackle these problems, a number of projects are targeting to produce larger plant-based alcohols with more than two carbon atoms per molecule such as butanol (four carbon atoms per molecule) and even as high as octanol (eight carbon atoms per molecule).

The approach taken by Codexis, a small California-based bioengineering company, is to engineer enzymes to produce octanol rather than ethanol. The field of enzyme modification to produce industrial chemicals called biocatalysis is developing quite rapidly. For example, Codexis has developed an enzyme to produce the chemical precursor for the production of the blockbuster cholesterol reducing drug, Lipitor.

Other young companies such as Avantium in the Netherlands are targeting to produce furanic-based biofuels (e.g. 2,5-dimethylfuran), which are more energy rich, less corrosive and not as volatile as ethanol.

10.11 Biodiesel from Algae

Algae offer the possibility of producing biodiesel from carbon dioxide, water, waste nutrients and highly efficient photosynthesis. This promising route to biodiesel from algae coupled with high crude oil prices has triggered a number of organizations to race for this potential prize.

For example, Shell Oil and HR Biopetroleum have recently announced a joint venture called Cellana to develop a demonstration facility to produce vegetable oil from algae. Marine algae have a number of advantages including rapid growth (double their mass several times per day), fifteen times higher yields per hectare than rape, palm soya or jatropha, and can be cultivated on coastal land unsuitable for conventional agriculture.

Scientists at the Universities of Hawaii, Southern Mississippi and Dalhousie in Canada screen natural algae species to discover those that produce the highest yields of vegetable oil. The demonstration plant is in open-air sea water ponds minimizing the use of fertile land and fresh water. Longer term algae cultivation facilities have the potential to "capture" waste CO_2 from industrial facilities such as power generation plants.

Other players in this field include A2BE Carbon Capture based in Boulder, Colorado, who are developing an algae technology to produce not only biodiesel but also animal feed protein and fertilizer in an integrated plant to improve the overall economics. This technology makes use of a photo-bioreactor for growing and harvesting the algae which consists of twin, transparent, plastic "algae water beds".

Algae-based biofuel process technology also has the potential to absorb carbon dioxide emissions from, for example, electric power plants and an Israeli company called Seambiotic is building a pilot plant with this application in mind. However, the carbon dioxide emissions from utility plants are so huge, it would require a highly efficient algae process to remove this enormous volume of carbon.

10.12 Third Generation Biofuels

Craig Venter, the maverick US scientist and founder of Synthetic Genomics, has announced that his company is working on the synthesis of a genome to create a new microbe that will behave like a "super algae". The remarkable recent feat of this research team in synthesizing the genome of the bacterium Mycoplasma genitalium provides some credibility to the possibility of achieving the major technical challenge.

This synthetic biocatalyst is being designed to efficiently convert carbon dioxide and sunlight into a high-octane hydrocarbon and represents the path to third generation biofuels. The microbe will be designed whereby the synthetic biofuel will diffuse through the cell walls enabling a relatively easy removal of the oil from the aqueous reaction mixture. Venter also claims that a process based on this synthetic microbe will be rapidly commercialized in less than 2 years. He envisages a future in which there could be as many as a million small bio-refineries scattered across the US producing biofuels based on this technology. Interestingly, the British oil giant BP and the high-profile venture capital firm Darper Fisher

Jurvetson are providing financial backing to Synthetic Genomics for this challenging project.

Researchers are also exploring the use of so-called extremophiles which are microbes that exist at high temperatures, often near underwater volcanoes. These organisms have the potential to operate as biocatalysts at relatively high temperatures with much increased reaction rates and therefore enhanced efficiency for biomass conversion.

A major breakthrough in this exciting field of biocatalyst carbon conversion technology would not only break the dependence on crude oil-based transportation fuels but may also provide an economically feasible process to absorb carbon dioxide from the atmosphere.

10.13 Bio-based Chemicals

The intense research activity related to biofuels has also triggered interest in converting biomass into high added value chemicals. Moreover, the current main building blocks of the chemical industry, such as ethylene and propylene, have experienced major price increases as they are produced from crude oil. Hence, in addition to sustainability, there is now also a compelling economic incentive to explore new routes to manufacture chemicals from biomass.

In fact, already there is a high level of interest to build plants to turn sugarcane produced ethanol into ethylene. For example, Dow Chemical, the US giant, is investing in Brazilian bioethylene facilities based on its confidence that the technology is ready for commercialization. Furthermore, Dow has developed a biomaterial made from soya bean oil that can be used in foam applications.

DuPont, another major US chemical company, expects its sales of industrial biotechnology products to grow by 16–18% a year reaching $1 billion by 2012. The company has already launched a new biofibre called Sorona, which they believe could potentially compete with nylon. Biopolymers, such as poly-lactic acid, are already being produced commercially and these biomaterials have an additional advantage over conventional crude oil derived polymers in that they are biodegradable. Cargill, the giant grain company, has also recently produced a biopolymer called Ingeo that will be used for food containers and textiles.

These new biomaterial developments have also attracted the attention of venture capital companies such as Khosla Ventures who have invested in a number of start-up companies focused in this area. These include companies such as Draths, Segetis and Soladigm who are targeting a wide range of biomaterials such as fine chemicals, surfactants, solvents, and biopolymers. Metabolix is another fledgling company that has started production of a biodegradable polymer.

This emerging field of biochemicals has the potential to be disruptive, potentially replacing some of the existing high-cost process technology based on crude oil with more economic and sustainable processes using biomass as a feedstock.

10.14 PV Solar

Photovoltaic (PV) solar energy has been around for some time and, while hold-ing high promise as a renewable energy source, the widespread adoption has been hindered by the relatively high cost. Many current applications rely quite heav-ily on government subsidies to make the projects economically feasible. However, the technology continues to drive down the incremental innovation cost curve and promises to deliver PV solar at very competitive prices by the year 2015 as shown in Fig. 10.4.

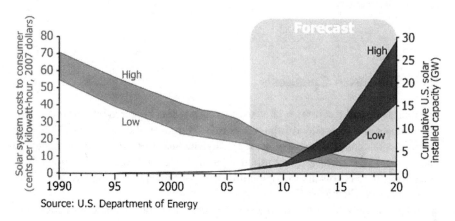

Fig. 10.4 Solar energy US forecasts for costs and installed capacity (Figure redrawn from source)

10.15 Thin-Film Solar

One of the major costs of PV solar is the polycrystalline silicon which is the core component of first generation technology. Second generation technologies make use of thin films of either silicon or alternative photoelectric materials to drive down the costs. According to the analyst firm, NanoMarkets, the market for thin-film photo-voltaics (TFPV) is one of the fastest growing technologies in the renewable energy sector. The thin film technology also has the advantage that the solar panels can be manufactured using flexible support materials as shown in Fig. 10.5. TFPV solar energy is predicted to rise dramatically to the equivalent of about 25 gigawatts by 2015 with a value of $20 billion in revenues.

Nanosolar is an example of a new PV solar company deploying innovative thin films of Copper Indium Gallium Diselenide (CIGS) as the photovoltaic semi-conductor component. They have developed nano-particles of these components that are combined to form a homogeneous ink that can be sprayed as a thin layer onto a

Fig. 10.5 Flexible rolls of thin film PV solar
panels (Source: Nanosolar)

flexible film support. Printing press style machines are used to create thin layers on
solar panels at a high rate dramatically reducing the production costs.

This innovative California-based company was only formed in 2002 and has
attracted $100 million in venture capital from the Google founders and well-known
Silicon Valley investors. They appear to have created quite a strong IP portfolio
with over 180 patents issued, licensed or pending. A world-scale solar thin film
manufacturing plant has been constructed in San Jose and a highly automated panel
assembly facility is based in Luckenwalde, Germany. Given the relatively short time
since the launch of the company, Nanosolar provides an excellent example of "speed
to market".

Nanosolar does appear to have significantly reduced both material and process
manufacturing costs and claims that, with their technology, solar power panels will
cost about $1 per watt, compared with conventional silicon-based PV at $3 per
watt. This would represent a quantum innovation and could lead to much more
widespread application of solar PV panels to generate electricity both domestically
and on an industrial scale. The recently launched Million Solar Roofs initiative in
California, with tax breaks and rebates, will likely accelerate the adoption of this
new solar technology.

Other players in CIGS solar technology include Heliovolt, Miasole, and Shell,
who are most likely still researching intensively to achieve sufficiently high solar
conversion efficiencies.

10.16 Solar Future

Solar energy is a field of intensive research with some promising technologies at the early stage of the innovation value chain. Some researchers are predicting that solar PV energy efficiencies could eventually increase from the current levels in the range of 15–20% to as high as 70%.

Perhaps, the most promising new generation technology involves concentrating and refracting light into different wavelengths and then deploying PV systems that are the most efficient for that particular part of the visible and even UV spectrum. Experimental systems utilizing this approach have already achieved solar efficiencies close to 50%. Assuming these technologies can be readily scaled up for manufacturing solar energy, costs will drop dramatically and solar could become highly competitive with coal-fired power generation.

10.17 Renewable Energy Storage

One of the major disadvantages of solar energy is the intermittent power generation. Another new company, called SolarReserve backed by United Technologies, aims to construct concentrated solar power towers similar to eSolar and store the energy in the form of heat in molten salts. The salts consist of a mixture of sodium and potassium nitrate that melt at high temperatures from the solar energy and this latent heat is then released as required through exchangers to produce steam and drive turbines to generate electrical power.

Deeya Energy is another Californian technology start-up dedicated to developing and manufacturing electrical energy storage systems based on its proprietary technology called L-Cell. These new, so-called flow batteries consist of large tanks containing dissolved electrolytes which are able to store power on an industrial scale. The technology is claimed to be three times cheaper than conventional lead-acid with a fast charging rate. Surprisingly, the new battery upstart A123 has also announced that they have signed with an electric utility company to use their high performance lithium-ion batteries to help stabilize the grid.

These recent quantum innovations in battery technology could potentially remove the fluctuations from solar and wind power generation. If successful, this would remove one of the major disadvantages of these renewable energy systems for both electric utility companies and home power generation.

10.18 Wind Power

Wind energy is plentiful, renewable, widely distributed, clean and reduces greenhouse gas emissions when it displaces fossil-fuel-derived electricity. The worldwide capacity of wind-powered generators was about 75 gigawatts at the end of 2006 having quadrupled since 2000. Although wind currently only produces just over 1% of world-wide electricity use, it accounts for about 20% of electricity production in Denmark, 9% in Spain, and 7% in Germany.

Wind power is mostly produced in large-scale so-called wind farms connected to electrical grids but is also used in the form of individual turbines for providing electricity to isolated locations such as rural farms.

Denmark is one of the most advanced countries in the world with the adoption of wind power with some 3 gigawatts of installed capacity in 2005 accounting for about 20% of the total electricity supply. Some of the wind turbines which are offshore as shown in Fig. 10.6.

Fig. 10.6 Offshore wind turbines near Copenhagen
(Source: Wikimedia commons)

Moreover, the Danes have been the most innovative in wind power research and development providing the basis for a vibrant EU 3 billion global business; Danish companies account for some 40% of the fast growing world turbine market. This provides an excellent example of a government with the foresight to provide a strong stimulus for innovation in a high potential growth business sector, enabling the development of a strong local experience base from which to expand into global markets.

The Danish wind power company, Vestas, is the global leader with 28% of the world market and some 33,000 wind turbines installed. Interestingly, a modern 3-MW wind turbine will replace 13,000 barrels of oil per year in terms of energy production.

China is also promoting wind energy as part of the goal to generate 5 gigawatts of electricity from clean energy by 2010. The largest Chinese wind energy company, Xinjiang Goldwind Science and Technology, is growing rapidly and has recently had a very successful IPO on the Shenzhen stock exchange.

The intermittency of wind is a disadvantage when using wind power to supply a significant proportion of total electrical demand. However, recent innovation in low-cost energy storage systems, as previously discussed, offers the potential to economically smooth the electricity production from wind farms.

Innovation in wind power has been largely incremental in driving down the experience curve to reduce capital costs. Some of the remaining issues with wind power include the noise factor, potential risk to bird life and the visual effects. In this regard vertical rather than the traditional horizontal axis wind turbines, such as the Darrieus design might offer some advantages, but due to other engineering drawbacks, this technology has not yet been able to penetrate significantly into the market.

Interestingly, the potential wind power available in the atmosphere around the globe is estimated to be much greater than current world energy consumption. However, the practical limit will likely be set by economic and environmental factors. Nevertheless, current predictions are that wind power will grow at the rate of 20% per annum reaching about 1,000 gigawatts by 2020.

10.19   Wave and Tidal Energy

Other renewable energy technologies such as wave and tidal power are under development but appear to face significant challenges in terms of scalability and robustness. Marine Current Turbines, who are based in the south of England, will soon complete their first "tidal farm" in Northern Ireland as shown in Fig. 10.7 and are planning to expand into North America.

Fig. 10.7 Marine Current turbines' tidal power design (Source: Marine Current turbines)

Perhaps the best known wave system is the "Sea Snake" as shown in Fig. 10.8, developed by Edinburgh-based Pelamis Wave Power, who have installed their first commercial system generating up to 750 kilowatts in Portugal and development for a second phase project is under-way.

Fig. 10.8 The Pelamis Wave Power "Sea Snake" (Source: Pelamis Wave Power)

The Pelamis technology generates electricity from turbines that are driven by hydraulic rams that are pumped by the wave motion at the hinged joints of the "sea snake". More wave farm projects using the Pelamis generators will likely be deployed in waters off Orkney in Scotland and Cornwall in the UK. Other novel wave technologies are tethered underwater buoys and limpets that oscillate with wave motion.

Clearly, innovation in the field of renewable energy is enjoying an almost explosive growth in funding from government grants, tax incentives and venture capital. These high levels of investment are already yielding some encouraging results and there will almost certainly be a wave of exciting renewable technologies reaching the market over the next few years. However, sustained innovation and massive capital investments will be required for these developments to attain sufficient scale that they will start to reduce the global dependence on fossil fuels and mitigate the effects of climate change.

Chapter 11
Clean Energy Innovation

The global energy market is massive with a current consumption level of close to 15,000 gigawatts of power worth some $6 trillion per year. Large and high GDP growth, developing countries such as India and China are adding new power generation facilities at rates and volumes that the world has never experienced before. For cost reasons, most of these new power generation facilities are currently based on coal as a fuel which, due its high level of impurities, makes it expensive to properly clean the off-gas emissions and, without this treatment, results in high levels of air pollution. In addition, coal is rich in carbon which means that the carbon dioxide greenhouse gas emissions from these plants are also relatively high. This has led to a sharp rise and continued increase in carbon dioxide (CO_2) emissions and climate change concerns, particularly from large and rapidly growing economies such as China and India as shown in Fig. 11.1.

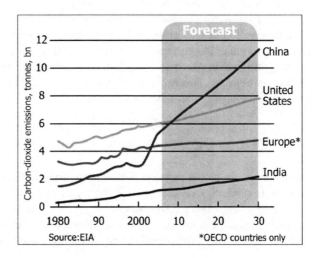

Fig. 11.1 The rapid rise in global carbon dioxide emissions (Redrawn from source)

I.E. Maxwell, *Managing Sustainable Innovation*,
DOI 10.1007/978-0-387-87581-1_11, © 2009 by Ian E. Maxwell

These global climate change concerns coupled with the recent dramatic increase in the price of oil and natural gas have almost certainly triggered the beginning of a transition from fossil-based fuels to a clean energy economy based on alternative and renewable sources. This transition will inevitably be slow given the massive size of the energy business as reflected in the past and shown in Fig. 11.2.

Fig. 11.2 Trends in the source of US energy supply (Redrawn from source)

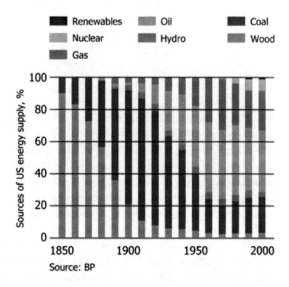

However, the speed of the research and development phase of these "green" technologies will likely be quite fast and create some exciting new innovative business opportunities. Interestingly, this alternative energy business opportunity is being recognized by venture capital companies, particularly in the US, where clean energy venture funds are currently booming.

Environmental awareness and sustainable growth are now also being embraced by many reputable companies around the world who place a high value on having a "green" image. For example, Wal-Mart, the world's largest public corporation by revenue, has recently announced a goal to work with suppliers to provide energy-efficient products in Wal-Mart stores targeting 25% more energy-efficiency within three years. This provides suppliers with a huge incentive to drive innovation towards low-energy consumption products.

11.1 Carbon Dioxide Capture

The man-made global increase in the concentration of carbon dioxide in the atmosphere is currently considered to be the major cause of global warming. To avoid potentially catastrophic effects of climate change, it is considered that global greenhouse gases should not be allowed to increase beyond 550 parts per million. To achieve this target, economically viable technology needs to be developed to remove carbon dioxide (sequestration) from the effluent gas streams of power plants and other major sources that burn fossil fuels.

While the developed world is largely responsible for the historical growth in greenhouse gases, the new fast-developing and highly populated countries such as China and India are now also becoming major contributors to global carbon dioxide emissions. Hence, carbon dioxide emissions from energy production have become an urgent global issue.

Coal is rich in carbon and coal-fired power stations are still a major global means of generating electricity; hence, an economic process to capture and store carbon dioxide (CCS) from these plants is highly desirable but poses major technological challenges. While the development and implementation of non-fossil fuel burning technologies such as solar, wind, hydro and geothermal energy are growing rapidly, this will most likely be insufficient to curb carbon dioxide emissions to remain below the climate change targets.

Hence a viable and cost-effective carbon sequestration technology that can also be retrofitted to existing fossil fuel plants is an urgent global technological and innovation challenge. Remarkably, there are relatively few projects of any significant size that are directly addressing this major problem. These projects include the Weyburn-Midale project which is storing carbon dioxide from a coal gasification plant in North Dakota in a depleted oil field in Saskatchewan. The English oil major, BP, is re-injecting CO_2 removed from natural gas back into the ground at the Salah gas field project in Algeria and Statoil, the Norwegian oil and gas company, is doing the same at two sites in the North Sea. Statoil has estimated that to apply its CCS technology to a coal or gas fired power station would increase the costs by about 50–80%. An ambitious project called Futurgen, which was being funded by the US Department of Energy (DOE), has been cancelled due to costs escalating to almost $2 billion.

The scale required for CCS technology to be globally successful is huge since electricity companies in the US alone produce some 1.5 billion tons of CO_2 per year. It seems unlikely that CCS technology will provide a convenient and cost-effective option to capture and store CO_2 from power stations. A process that chemically converts CO_2 into useful products would potentially be much more cost effective. In this regard, the development of algae processes which use CO_2 and sunlight to produce biofuels might hold promise in the future if sufficient scale can be achieved. The highly venturesome approach of Synthetic Genomics, led by Craig Venter, to engineer new genes that produce algae that will expel oil from their membranes might provide a breakthrough in this regard. The follow-up to the Kyoto agreement and the introduction of carbon taxes that is being contemplated by the US and other countries could further spur innovation in CO_2 conversion technology.

11.2 Electric Vehicles

The convergence of a number of powerful global forces has regenerated a high level of interest in "plug-in" electric vehicles. These mega trends include the dramatic price increase in crude oil based automotive fuels, global climate change concerns due to greenhouse gas emissions, and urban pollution levels caused by motor vehicles. To date, the major technical limitation to the adoption of electric vehicles has been the storage capacity and weight of battery systems. These battery limitations have severely limited the power and distance that electric vehicles can travel before the batteries need recharging. The so-called hybrid vehicles such as the Toyota Prius, which are powered by a combination of conventional combustion engines and electric motors, do not suffer from this distance limitation but also do not provide the many advantages of a fully electric motor powered car.

However, recent advances in battery systems and, in particular, those based on lithium-ion technology have contributed to a surge of interest in "plug-in" electric vehicles. For example, A123 has developed a new lithium-ion battery based on nano-particles of lithium iron phosphate modified with trace metals. These novel batteries have much faster charging times and have about double the power density of current similar battery systems. In addition, they are also much more robust than conventional lithium-ion batteries and A123 is predicting that they will last longer than the typical lifetime of a car.

General Motors (GM), for example, is currently testing the A123 batteries for their new Volt electric vehicle which is expected to go into mass production as early as 2010. This interest in electric vehicles is not limited to GM; other major automobile manufacturers such as Toyota, Honda, Mitsubishi and Nissan, all have plans to develop fully electric vehicles.

Further, an alliance between Nissan and Renault has recently announced plans to launch an all-electric car in the US and Japan by 2010 and envisions having a broad range of such vehicles in the future with the ambition to be the world leader in zero-emission cars. The Renault-Nissan electric vehicles will be equipped with lithium-ion batteries supplied by Nissan's joint venture with NEC.

In addition to the advanced technology required to produce an efficient and cost-effective electric car, there will be major investments needed in the infrastructure to support these new vehicle developments. In this regard, Nissan-Renault, for example, has formed a partnership with Project Better Place, an Israeli electric vehicle infrastructure company, who plan to invest up to $1 billion in parking meter charging stations and battery replacement facilities. Israel is a good fit for such a network since 90% of Israeli car owners drive less than 70 km per day and the government has recently extended a tax incentive on the purchase of any "zero-emissions vehicle" until 2019. Interestingly, Project Better Place is also in discussions with the city of San Francisco to potentially provide the infrastructure for a fleet of plug-in cars.

Electric cars have the potential to generate disruptive innovation in the automobile industry whereby traditional players could be threatened and new players enter the market. Examples of new players in this emerging market might be the low cost Indian car manufacturers such as Tata Motors (the creator of the Nano car) and Mahindra and Mahindra who are already planning to produce hybrid vehicles.

Another interesting player is a Norwegian company called Think that recently unveiled a small, affordable, electric car named Ox that can travel between 125 and 155 miles before recharging. The Ox also makes use of the state-of-the-art lithium-ion batteries produced by A123. A solar panel on the roof keeps the vehicle's interior cool when the engine is switched off, or can even supply enough power to run the sound system on the beach. Think is targeting the North American market and has received funding from some big VC names in Silicon Valley such as Rockport Capital Partners and Kleiner Perkins Caufield & Byers. An innovative lean manufacturing model has been adopted by Think which has a supply chain that resembles that of Dell, the PC company and dramatically reduces the capital costs of the assembly plant.

Clearly, all these developments support the notion that electric vehicles have very likely reached a "tipping point" and will rapidly gain in popularity and market share within a relatively short time frame.

11.3 Honda Hydrogen Home Station

Hydrogen is potentially a very attractive clean fuel since the only product from combustion is water. However, hydrogen is expensive to produce and, being a very light gas, it is difficult to store. Nevertheless, Honda and its technology partner, Plug Power, have developed a Home Energy Station which generates hydrogen from natural gas. This clean hydrogen fuel is then used to provide heat and electricity for the home as well as fuel for a zero emission hydrogen-powered fuel cell vehicle, such as the Honda FCX. However, currently both the capital costs of the hydrogen generation and the fuel cells are high which will likely retard the widespread adoption of this clean technology solution.

11.4 "Clean" Lighting

Lighting accounts for about 20% of all power consumption and conventional incandescent bulbs are very inefficient, producing large amounts of waste heat. The recent, rapid increase in global electricity costs has created a strong trend towards much more efficient lighting systems. Fortunately, recent technology innovation has led to a marked decrease in the costs of more efficient light bulbs offering new cost-effective ways of reducing waste heat. Compact fluorescent (CFL) and light emitting diode (LED) lights offer very significant lifetime economic advantages over the conventional incandescent systems.

These cost-effective, energy-saving lighting innovations have prompted a number of countries such as the EU and the US to introduce new legislation to phase out the energy-hungry incandescent light bulbs by 2012. It would seem to be very likely that many other countries will adopt similar policies offering the world a "cleaner" lighting future.

Although solid state LED technology has been around since the 1960s, only recently have the costs come down sufficiently to allow them to compete with conventional lighting. Moreover, the price of LEDs is continuing to decrease by about a half every 18 months.

A string of new products based on LEDs is therefore suddenly hitting the market. These semiconductors use a fraction of the energy compared to conventional lighting and can be battery powered. The multinational lighting companies such as Osram, GE and Philips are all racing to launch new innovative LED products as shown in Fig. 11.3.

Fig. 11.3 Energy efficient LED lights (Source: Wikimedia commons)

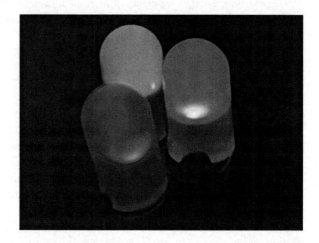

The lighting giants are also adapting their business models to compensate for the much longer life of the LED lights. Philips, for example, has recently spent $4.3 billion purchasing some five companies in the lighting sector including companies such as Genlyte. This has enabled Philips to command a strong position in the LED value chain and become a provider of complete lighting solutions to large, professional customers. The shift towards more efficient lighting has reinvigorated the lighting division of Philips to become a $9 billion business with high future growth.

Since LEDs are some 40% more efficient than conventional incandescent bulbs, Philips believes that Europe could meet its 2010 Kyoto carbon dioxide targets simply by switching to these energy efficient lighting alternatives. Such large, carbon-saving incentives will undoubtedly lead to significant further innovation and technology diffusion in the lighting business in the future.

A company called d.light design based in New Delhi, India, has developed a low-cost LED for the huge market of 1.6 billion low-income people at the without access to regular electricity. This innovative portable Nova light has a high-powered LED that can run on batteries for 40 hours on a full charge. It comes with a solar panel, so recharging costs nothing. Currently, many people in India and Africa without electricity use kerosene lanterns as a light source which emits unhealthy fumes, is an extremely dim light and often ends up burning people or homes in accidents.

Hence, the Nova LED light offers an affordable, safe and clean lighting solution to these low-income people.

11.5 The Zero Carbon City

It seems almost ironic that Abu Dhabi, with some 100 billion barrels in oil reserves, is planning to build a new energy innovative city, called Masdar ("the source" in Arabic) which will be the world's first metropolis that will not emit carbon dioxide.

Masdar, which is being designed by the London-based architects Foster and Partners and is expected to cost $22 billion, will incorporate the most advanced technology available to generate power which will depend largely on solar energy. The array of technologies will include thin-film solar panels that serve as the facades and roofing materials for buildings, ubiquitous sensors for monitoring energy use and driverless vehicles powered by batteries that make cars unnecessary. The city will also incorporate design features based on traditional Arabic architecture using wind towers to funnel air through the streets and fountains to dampen the dry desert heat.

Indeed, the city's founders hope that it will serve as a test bed for a myriad of new technologies being proposed to reduce greenhouse gas emissions. The vision is that Abu Dhabi will one day run out of oil and the emirate is investing heavily into renewable and sustainable energy technologies as part of their long-term economic strategy. Other components of this Masdar Initiatives strategy include the founding of a research university in partnership with MIT called the Masdar Institute, which will specialize in renewable technologies, a $250 million Clean Technology Fund and a special economic zone for the advanced energy industry.

The recent announcement by Abu Dhabi to build a huge 500 MW solar power plant confirms their ambitions to become a serious player in the solar energy business sector. Masdar executives are predicting that within a decade, they will have developed world class expertise in solar energy, photovoltaics, energy storage, carbon sequestration and hydrogen fuel systems. Indeed, the Masdar Initiative may have the potential to become the "Silicon Valley" of renewable energy in the future.

11.6 Chinese Eco-city

China has also made a serious commitment to sustainability with the announcement of the Dongtan eco-city project. This project is a new low-energy consumption and carbon-neutral city planned for the island of Chongming at the mouth of the Yangtze River near Shanghai. This new eco-city is planned to open with accommodation for some 10,000 visitors in time for the Expo 2010. Dongtan is one of up to four such cities to be designed and built in China by Arup, a global design and engineering company. These cities are planned to be ecologically friendly with zero carbon emission transit systems whereby the only vehicles allowed in the cities will be powered by electricity or hydrogen. Dongtan will produce its own energy from wind, solar, biofuel and recycled city waste. By 2040, the city is slated to have a population of some 500,000.

11.7 Geothermal Energy

Geothermal is a source of clean energy that uses the heat energy of the earth to generate power with almost no greenhouse gas emissions. The multinational energy company, Chevron, has predicted that geothermal energy could potentially be used to produce some 10% of global power requirements. The geologic conditions conducive to generating power from geothermal energy exist in certain parts of the world such as the Pacific Rim.

In geographical locations where deep fractures occur in the earth's crust, molten material, or magma, pushes close enough to the surface to heat water that naturally seeps deep into the earth. Areas around inactive volcanoes are generally the most productive for geothermal energy. Under the right conditions, an underground reservoir can be tapped by drilling a well in a similar manner to those used to recover crude oil and natural gas. As the steam from the wells rises to the surface, the pressure decreases and it expands. This steam is then used to drive turbines which produce electricity. The residual is re-injected into the reservoir and the cycle of energy is renewed. Currently California, Iceland, Italy, the Philippines, New Zealand and Japan are the geographies where geothermal energy is used for power generation on a significant scale.

In Iceland, there are five major geothermal power plants which in 2006 produced about 26% of the country's electricity. In addition, geothermal heating meets the heating and hot water requirements for around 87% of the nation's housing. Due to government foresight, Iceland is now in the very fortunate position that geothermal and hydroelectric power account for almost all of the electricity generation with only 0.1 % coming from fossil fuels.

Fig. 11.4 Geothermal power plant in Iceland (Source: Wikimedia commons)

Innovation in geothermal energy is undergoing a revival with a focus on advanced drilling technology to exploit new fields and the efficient use of lower quality steam to expand the global application of geothermal power. This growth potential is already reflected in US companies focused on geothermal power generation such as Raser Technologies and Ormat Technologies whose stocks have recently made substantial gains.

An exciting new development in this energy field is the so-called engineered geothermal system (EGS) which is based on drilling two parallel holes in the ground, a few hundred metres apart, and carry on drilling until the rock is hot enough (say 200°C). Cold water is pumped down one hole and superheated water returns up the other hole which turns to steam at the surface and is used to power a generator.

Experts believe that the recoverable heat in underground rock, for example, under the United States is the equivalent of 2,000 years-worth of the country's current energy consumption. However, extracting this subterranean energy is not as easy as might be expected, since impermeable rocks such as granite are the most effective reservoirs of heat but to effectively transfer this heat to cold water, they need to be permeable. Research and development is therefore required to find ways to force open fissures in the granite to enhance the flow of water from the injection hole to the exit.

The Cooper Basin in South Australia has the hottest non-volcanic rocks of any known place in the world, and Australia leads the field in exploiting subterranean heat. One company called Geodynamics has recently completed what it claims is a commercial-scale well. This EGS technology makes use of a loop that operates under pressure where the super-heated water remains a liquid. The high temperatures of the geothermal hot water are transferred to the power station loop via a heat exchanger. This form of geothermal energy relies on the presence of high heat production granites. The heat is trapped inside these granites by an overlying blanket of insulating rocks. Such a blanket has to be about 3 km thick for the required temperatures in excess of 200°C to be generated. The future of this promising EGS technology will likely depend on the abundance and accessibility of suitable, high-temperature granite structures within the earth's crust.

Clean technology is enjoying a revival driven by high energy costs and climate change concerns. Energy efficiency is now high on the agendas of many governments around the world. Electric vehicles are moving rapidly towards a "tipping point" as a new generation Li-ion batteries hold promise to markedly improve their performance. Geothermal power is expanding in the Pacific Rim and the new EGS technology offers some exciting prospects for clean energy in the future. The investment in new low emission cities in the United Arab Emirates and China will provide some interesting experiments in large scale urban application of both clean and renewable technologies.

Chapter 12
IT Innovation

Information technology (IT) has probably been the business sector with the most dynamic level of innovation in the past decade. The rapid developments of both hardware and software, in the form of business solutions, have enabled companies and organizations around the globe to achieve major gains in productivity. The microchips that are the powerhouses of computers have continued to follow the well-established Moore's Law, whereby computing power doubles every 18 months. Software development has rapidly absorbed this growth in computing power and ever more sophisticated programmes are able to handle increasingly complex tasks, including the mega networks of so-called Cloud computing.

Some examples include the rapid computation of 3D images from non-invasive medical diagnostic tools such as CAT and MRI scans; the computer-assisted design of new drug molecules using 3D computer simulations; computer-aided design and manufacturing of highly complex products such as the new Airbus Superjumbo A380 and the Boeing 787 aircraft. Fully integrated software systems established between parts suppliers and manufacturers have enabled companies such as Dell Computers to develop new business models with a dramatic reduction in working capital.

Moreover, the Internet has now transformed global communications and created new disruptive business models as exemplified by the search and online advertising giant, Google.

12.1 Cyberspace Innovation

The meteoric rise of Google from its humble beginnings in 1996 as a PhD research project of two Stanford students, Larry Page and Sergey Brin, to a dynamic global company with a current market capital of about $100 billion, is a reflection of the massive technological and commercial impact of cyberspace on the global management of information and knowledge. Other examples include the rapid growth of social networks, such as YouTube, which enables the rapid, world-wide exchange of information and communication, including digital photos and video. The global

I.E. Maxwell, *Managing Sustainable Innovation*,
DOI 10.1007/978-0-387-87581-1_12, © 2009 by Ian E. Maxwell

reach and power of this new medium for communication is reflected in the recent
launch of her own channel on YouTube by the Queen of England.

12.2 Global Geobrowsing

A US company called Keyhole developed the first commercial virtual earth software
to enable "geobrowsing" through the Internet in 2001, which was purchased by
Google in 2004 and launched as Google Earth in 2005, as shown in Fig. 12.1.

Google Earth contains overlaying maps of the entire world derived from a patch-
work of satellite imagery and aerial photography. The US space agency, NASA, has
a similar product called World Wind, and Microsoft bought GeoTango to create Virtual Earth, yet another web-based geobrowser. Virtual Earth continues to add detail
in the form of 3D models of cities rendered from aerial photography; so far, some
14 million gigabytes of data have been accumulated on 900 servers.

Like many new innovative technologies, geobrowsing, in addition to producing
stunning images of the globe that can be zoomed in and out, is finding some unex-
pected applications. Google Earth, for example, was used to coordinate the relief

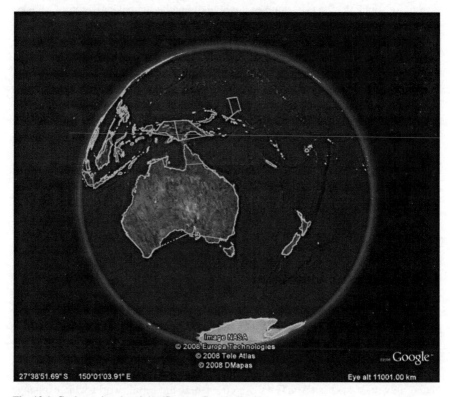

Fig. 12.1 Geobrowsing the globe (Source: Google Earth)

effort in 2005 in the aftermath of Hurricane Katrina in the New Orleans area. New historic sites have been discovered; landscape gardeners and solar panel installers are aided to search for target customers; city council planners can better evaluate new building developments; this list continues to grow.

The potential for new innovation through these virtual earth media has caught the interest of investors and many geospatial companies have recently been the target of mergers and acquisitions. However, as the spatial resolution and detail of geo-browsing continues to improve, there are increasing concerns with regard to military security and invasion of privacy which will need to be addressed.

A subsequent phase of innovation involves the merging of satellite global positioning (GPS) technology with geobrowsing and a new company called Socialight is focusing on this concept, offering to mobile phone users with built-in GPS technology the possibility of attaching notes to any location on a geobrowser map as they travel. Clearly, this could mark the beginning of a whole new array of real-time experience applications of these global-based technologies.

12.3 Amazon's Kindle

The recent launch of the new electronic book reader, Kindle, by Jeff Bezos, the flamboyant CEO of the Internet commerce giant, Amazon, has created renewed interest in e-books. This novel gadget might just be the quantum innovation required to challenge the age-old paper book as shown in Fig. 12.2.

Fig. 12.2 Kindle e-Book (Source: Wikimedia commons)

The e-ink technology used in the device makes it possible to achieve the clarity of a printed book and, hence, very readable pages. The battery life provides 30 hours of reading, with storage for some 200 books which is extendable with a memory card. Perhaps, the most interesting feature is the wireless connection to the Internet using a system called Whispernet that provides access to a huge virtual library provided by Amazon that can be downloaded for $9.99 per best seller book. The vision of Jeff Bezos is that anyone should be able to access any book that has ever been in print, in less than a minute by means of the Kindle device.

In addition to books, subscriptions to newspapers and magazines are also available through the web-based e-book. The question arises as to whether this technology signals the beginning of the death of the printed book – a possibility – although the transition will likely be very long.

12.4 Cloud Computing

Christophe Bisciglia, a young engineer at Google, posed the challenge as to what people would do with 1,000 times more data than they currently manage. This challenge addresses the global growing issue of scale as computing capability expands rapidly, producing ever increasing amounts of raw data and information that needs to be processed and transformed into knowledge. The concept of Cloud computing comprises a network of many hundreds of thousands of servers all linked together, with the supporting software to store and manage huge amounts of data. Traditional supercomputers have similar capabilities but the cloud can both regenerate and grow, as servers in the vast network are replaced and expanded, creating an almost living system that does not age.

In fact, the Google network of servers is itself a cloud that stores copies of the complete World Wide Web and has highly advanced software for managing their search services, their advertising business and their e-mail service. Google is continuously expanding and renewing their cloud, adding, for example, four new data centres in 2007 at a cost of about $600 million each. The Google cloud is the core technology platform of their powerful business model which provides another excellent example of a quantum innovation.

Based on the initiative of Bisciglia, the cloud concept was launched as the Google 101 project and is designed to replicate the Google cloud and make this available as a living super computer to external users. In fact, IBM was so intrigued by the cloud concept that they have formed a partnership with Google to prototype this concept. Cloud computing is first being launched with a number of US universities where researchers will have access to enormous computing capacity. The participating universities include the University of California at Berkeley, MIT, Stanford, Carnegie Mellon, the University of Washington and the University of Maryland.

In addition, university computer scientists will have the opportunity to further develop and enhance the software tools and applications that make the Cloud so highly effective and functional. After a trial period with the universities, the Cloud system is expected to be offered globally and will offer these "living" super computing capabilities to scientists, engineers and businesses around the world.

Parallel computing technology, where a task is divided into many thousands of smaller tasks that are executed in parallel, will also get a major boost from these cloud developments. In fact, the core software in the Google Cloud, called MapReduce, is based on parallel computing technology which is highly suited to massive networks of computers.

This exciting Cloud computing development has the potential to create a more level playing field for many types of business, providing them with access to supercomputers that have until now been available only to the Internet and IT giants. Potentially, this broad access to Cloud computing could spawn new start-up companies not only in IT but also for science-based businesses such as drug discovery, where tools such as molecular modelling using supercomputers is becoming increasingly important.

12.5 Microsoft Versus Google

A remarkable battle is emerging between the two IT giants, Microsoft and Google, that will have a major impact on the delivery of application software in the future. The Microsoft business is based on the traditional model whereby software is sold to customers for a license fee, ongoing improvements and upgrades commanding additional fees. A dominant market share for PC computing is captured by incorporating the Microsoft operating system and basic application software in the sale of new computers. More than 500 million people around the globe are using Microsoft software through this delivery mode.

Google and other smaller players are now challenging this business model by offering software applications that are delivered through the web. This means that the application computer code resides on the server of the software company, rather than on the user's own computer. These online software products, so-called "software as a service" (SaaS), are not subject to the traditional long build, test and shipping cycles of software development, since the web-based software can be delivered and updated through the web providing an ideal model for "speed to market". For example, Google has updated its e-mail system, its online applications such as spreadsheets, word processing, presentations and its new cell phone software in just months rather than years. For small businesses, this software online model can also substantially reduce their internal IT support service costs. The growth of this business model is reflected in the fact that some 2,000 small business companies are signing up for Google applications each working day.

Clearly, Cloud computing has the potential to provide even relatively small companies with access to supercomputing power and highly advanced software tools, at relatively low cost through the Internet. Even large corporations are starting to move to Google applications such as Gmail, to provide the services needed to handle large volumes of e-mail traffic and spam. Arizona State University with 65,000 students has decided to move to Gmail and so effectively outsource the IT services required to support this large number of student users. As a further benefit, the students have access to the Google word processing, spread sheet and calendar applications.

All these rapidly developing web-based software solutions are severely challenging the traditional Microsoft licensing business model. The past massive $44 billion bid by Microsoft for the Internet giant, Yahoo, was a clear reflection that they are yielding to this new business approach. Somewhat surprisingly, the original online book company, Amazon, is also moving into Cloud computing and offering large amounts of data storage and data management services for a fee. This is an interesting example of an IT company that is expanding its business model into data services, based on core competencies developed for an online sales business.

Cloud computing and online software are exciting new quantum, or possibly even disruptive, innovations that have the potential to provide supercomputing capabilities and highly advanced software applications to both small and large businesses around the globe.

12.6 Apple's iPhone

Mobile phones are destined to have a bright future with about a billion people around the world using this technology as a prime means of interpersonal communication. Following the successful introduction of the first touch technology iPhone in mid-2007, Apple has more recently launched a new and cheaper 3G network model with a built-in Global Positioning System (GPS) and enhanced computing power and memory.

In addition, Apple released a software developer's kit (SDK) in advance of this launch to enable independent companies to create new applications for the iPhone. This has led to a surge of software development creating new applications that have turned the iPhone into, for example, a game console, a musical instrument, a navigation tool, a web browser device and a medical imaging viewer as shown in Fig. 12.3.

This new trend towards open innovation around mobile phone software development has major implications for this industry and poses a threat to other players with a closed software innovation business model such as Nokia.

The iPhone may also have far reaching implications for the wider use of the mobile Web for advertising and hence also poses a threat to companies like Google. It is, therefore, not surprising that Google has launched an Open Handset Alliance (OHA) to design a new operating system, code-named Android, which would provide an open platform for cell phone users. Google hope that Android will provide a cheaper and more open mobile software platform that will stimulate novel web applications and thereby enhance their advertising revenue stream.

As web screens become much smaller on mobile handsets, Google wants to influence what fits on these tiny screens. Clearly, all these players foresee the huge potential for free software applications via mobile phones, supported by advertising

Fig. 12.3 Apple's touch technology iPhone
(Source: Wikimedia commons)

revenues. Already, new web sites known as ad networks track consumer behaviour across multiple sites, and then shoot targeted ads to users. This behavioural targeting approach will very likely also move onto mobile web devices.

12.7 Microsoft's Surface

Microsoft has recently launched a new technology called Surface, which is a touch-sensitive table that could possibly redefine the way people interact with machines as shown in Fig. 12.4. This innovative technology has been running hot and cold in the Microsoft research labs for some five years prior to this market launch.

The Surface technology takes advantage of people's natural sense of touch and spatial orientation, offering more precise control over what's happening on the screen than pointing and clicking with a mouse. Further, the systems can incorporate familiar objects such as toys, game tokens and cell phones into the computing experience. The broader usefulness of Surface computing remains to be seen, since the current applications appear to be somewhat limited. In addition, the success of

Fig. 12.4 Microsoft's
surface technology
(Source: Microsoft)

tactile computing may depend in large part on how willing the users are to adapt to a new computer interface technology.

However, the success of the Apple iPhone, which employs advanced touch technology, may indicate that this form of human machine interaction does indeed have high potential for the future.

12.8 Search

The explosive growth of Internet use and the massive amounts of information now potentially accessible anywhere in the world means that powerful search tools are becoming extremely important. While the Google search tools are currently dominant, the technology is still relatively simple in the sense that only words or groups of words are searched, without any intelligence around their meaning.

For example, pharmaceutical company scientists developing new drugs need to sift through vast amounts of data such as scientific papers, clinical trials and gene research. In addition, with new fast DNA sequencing machines becoming available, many terabytes of data are being generated for each gene analyzed. The demand for powerful new search tools will escalate to enable the analysis of these huge genetic data bases for the development of, for example, personalized medicine and improved medical diagnostics.

These current search limitations have prompted the development of new, so-called, semantic web technology that is able to search and analyze the actual meaning of words and phrases to produce more meaningful results. Large companies such as Google, Yahoo, Adobe, Oracle and HP are actively developing Semantic Web technology. In addition, a number of start-up companies such as Powerset, Radar Networks, Hakia and Zoominfo have business models focused on these advanced search tools. The recent announcement that Microsoft has purchased Powerset for a rumoured price of around $100 million provides a good measure of the growing importance of semantic web technology. Almost certainly, other acquisitions will follow as the IT giants, who are currently building big server farms, ensure that they remain at the cutting edge of search technology.

However, the semantic web has some hurdles to overcome such as the much greater processing power required for the searches and the major task of re-indexing the entire web. To date, most of the semantic technologies have only been tested on data bases such as Wikipedia.

Eventually, advanced search tools will likely have built-in artificial intelligence that will continually learn as information is gathered from the web. Such developments should lead to search systems that will generate knowledge rather than gather information.

12.9 Smart Robots

Robot technology continues to steadily advance in terms of both capabilities and lower costs relative to the average price of human labour, providing a good example of incremental innovation as shown in Fig. 12.5.

Fig. 12.5 The decreasing relative cost of industrial robots (Redrawn from source)

Average robot prices relative to labour compensation

1990 - 100

Source: International Federation of Robotics

These trends are such that the number of industrial robots that are carrying out laborious manufacturing tasks such as cutting, welding and assembling has now reached about 1 million. Single-function robots are now penetrating into the home for tasks such as vacuum cleaning, lawn mowing and providing security. Perhaps, more importantly, a new generation of intelligent robots with humanoid-like characteristics is now emerging from laboratories such as the Toyota robot shown in Fig. 12.6.

Fig. 12.6 Toyota humanoid robot
(Source: Wikimedia commons)

These humanoid robots make use of major advances in various disciplines such as software, optics, electronics, computers, sensors and mechanics. Service robots have a bright future in developing countries where the demographic trends are creating a large population of elderly people needing home support. It now seems likely that humanoid robots will be providing support services to enable the aging baby boomers to enjoy the freedom of their own homes for a great deal longer.

The IT business sector has fully recovered from the bursting of the dot.com bubble and a surge of new innovations based on more robust business models are successfully reaching the market. Moreover, the Internet has become ubiquitous with new software applications that exploit the global interconnectivity offered by this powerful cyberspace medium. Already, the next generation of high-speed wireless technologies, called 4G and LTE, is being launched with the potential to penetrate beyond mobile phones and laptops, into digital cameras and smart electricity meters. Cloud computing is poised to become the preferred mode of managing data and delivering software as a service to customers. High speed computing is on the verge of displacing 2D with 3D images for a wide variety of applications. Artificial intelligence may be finally emerging in the form of humanoid robots that could soon be providing household support to the aging baby boomers.

Chapter 13
Healthcare Innovation

Innovation in the health sector has been quite phenomenal over the past few decades as evidenced by rapid development of new drugs, medical devices and health management software underpinned by world class scientific research. However, these spectacular healthcare innovations have been accompanied by ever increasing costs to governments, hospitals, medical insurance companies and patients. In addition, poor countries are demanding that life-saving drugs be made available at much lower cost for humane reasons.

In addition to this cost issue, large pharmaceutical companies are faced with many blockbuster drugs coming off patent, being withdrawn from the market due to severe side effects and relatively weak pipelines of new drugs from their own large research laboratories. Parallel to these political and business developments, scientific biological research continues to make great strides in gaining a deeper understanding of human biology at the molecular level as witnessed by the recent major advances in gene technology. The convergence of these powerful global forces is creating some major challenges for both innovation and business development in the healthcare sector.

13.1 Blockbuster Blues

Most therapeutic drugs are provided in the form of tablets that are taken orally by the patient and are composed of so-called small molecules containing about 100 atoms. The development of these small-molecule drugs has provided the basis for the modern pharmaceutical industry. Examples of modern multi-billion dollar blockbuster drugs include Lipitor (Pfizer)and Zocor (Merck) for cholesterol lowering, Norvasc (Pfizer) for hypertension, Zoloft (Pfizer), Zyprexa (Eli Lilly) for schizophrenia, Effexor (Wyeth) for depression, Plavix (Bristol-Myers Squid) for thrombosis, Nexium (AstraZeneca) for gastrointestinal disorders and, more recently, Viagra (Pfizer)and Cialis (Eli Lilly) for erectile dysfunction.

Small molecule drugs normally derive their therapeutic properties by interacting with the sites of disease, which are often proteins, in the human body as shown in Fig. 13.1. However, this interaction is not always highly selective and the drugs tend

I.E. Maxwell, *Managing Sustainable Innovation*,
DOI 10.1007/978-0-387-87581-1_13, © 2009 by Ian E. Maxwell

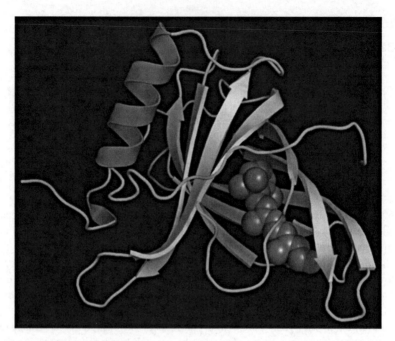

Fig. 13.1 A small biologically active molecule, refinol interacting with a protein
(Source: Wikimedia Commons)

to also interact with other healthy parts of the human biology and produce unwanted side effects which may vary significantly from one patient to another.

A recent notable example of undesired side effects is Vioxx, a drug developed by Merck, which was very effective in reducing pain for arthritis sufferers but was later discovered, in some cases, to increase the risk of heart attacks and strokes and was voluntarily withdrawn from the market in 2004. This cardiotoxicity of Vioxx is now thought to be due to the suppression of an anti-clotting agent in the blood.

Vioxx was a $2.5 billion dollar blockbuster drug for Merck who has also faced a large volume of individual and class action litigation. Further, Merck has recently withdrawn a successor drug called Prexige, due to side effects of severe liver damage. Other examples of withdrawn drugs include a high density (HDL) "good" cholesterol increasing drug called Torcetrapib developed by Pfizer, which, in late stage clinical trials, was shown to have a side effect of fatal heart attacks. Bayer was forced to withdraw Baycol, a "bad" cholesterol reducing drug in 2001, due to muscle cell breakdown side effects; and Wyeth withdrew Redux, a diet drug used to treat obesity, when patients showed abnormally high levels of heart valve disease.

These serious side effects, which generally only occur in a small proportion of patients, are most likely due to minor differences in the genetic make-up of individual patients. Unfortunately, medical science is not yet able to prescreen the individual genes of each patient in advance to determine the propensity towards acute drug side effects. However, it is quite probable that such genetic prescreening will be available sometime in the future which could lead to a revival of some small-molecule drugs that have been withdrawn from the market.

Big pharma companies are not only faced with the challenges of unpredictable side effects but the patent protection of many blockbuster drugs is expiring. This opens the path for other smaller companies that specialize in pharmaceutical manufacturing to also bring these so-called generic drugs to market. Generic drugs, due to competition, command much lower prices than proprietary drugs which results in a dramatic drop in the prices of what were previously blockbusters. Pfizer, for example, will likely lose some $13 billion per year when Lipitor goes off-patent in 2010.

To further exacerbate the situation, the research & development pipelines of big pharma are not heavily loaded with new potential blockbuster drugs, often referred to as the "pharmaceutical innovation gap". All these negative factors have raised the question as to the future viability of the blockbuster business model. Hence, pharmaceutical companies are reexamining their traditional business and innovation models in search of future sustainable revenues and growth. This includes moving, through acquisitions, into the realm of large biological drug molecules that has until recently been the domain of biotechnology companies.

Examples include the purchase of MedImmune by Astra Zeneca for $16 billion, the purchase of Sirna Therapeutics by Merck for $1.1 billion, Abbott Laboratories' takeover of Kos Pharmaceuticals for $3.7 billion and Novartis recently bought MorphoSys for $1 billion. Pharmaceutical acquisitions also include medical device and diagnostic companies indicative of a convergence of healthcare technologies which could well stimulate innovation through cross-fertilization.

13.2 Bright Biologics

The field of molecular biology was pioneered by Watson and Crick with their famous discovery in 1953 of the double helix structure of deoxyribonucleic acid (DNA) for which they received the Nobel prize. DNA is the basic building block that defines all aspects of a living organism. Watson and Crick revealed that DNA is made up of two strands, each having a chain of four types of nucleotide bases, adenine (A), thymine (T), cytosine (C), and guanine (G) as shown in Fig. 13.2, which are attached to a supporting scaffold of sugar and phosphate molecules.

DNA molecules provide the genetic code for the production of proteins which are responsible for all the biochemical activity in a living being.

Major advances in molecular biology in recent years have enabled the development of a whole new class of drugs based on much larger molecules (e.g. proteins) with many tens or even hundreds of thousands of atoms (macromolecules) which closely resemble the biological building blocks of humans. These so-called biologics, although much more complex as shown in Fig. 13.3, tend to interact much more

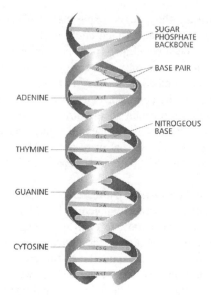

Fig. 13.2 DNA double helix structure
(Source: Wikimedia Commons)

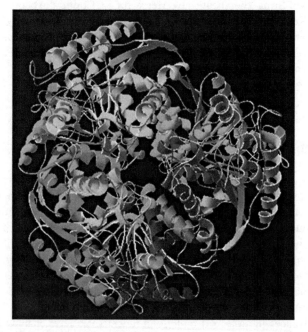

Fig. 13.3 Molecular structures of biological drugs
(Source: Wikimedia Commons)

selectively with the sites of disease and, therefore, result in more potent drugs often with fewer side effects.

Genetic engineering has provided the technical foundation for the rapid emergence of biological drugs. These so-called recombinant DNA techniques (rDNA) enable cells to be engineered to produce mass quantities of either new or existing proteins for use as new drug molecules.

Biologics has already created new multinational, so-called, biotechnology companies such as, Genetech and Amgen, which specialize in the research, development and marketing of macromolecule-based drugs with multi-billion dollar annual revenues and market capitalizations to match. Some of the therapeutic successes of biologic drugs include Epogen for anaemia and cancer (Amgen), Enbrel for rheumatoid arthritis (Amgen), Herceptin and Rituxan for cancer (Genetech) and Pulmozyme for cystic fibrosis (Genetech).

Further advances in molecular biology involving the structure and function of genes and proteins have led to new companies that specialize in genomics and proteomics, respectively. Successful genomic companies include Affymetrics, Celera Genomics, Incyte genomics and Millennium, while some notable proteomics companies include Ciphergen, Caliper, Lynx, Nanogen and Paradigm Genetics.

Biotechnology companies have now sprouted all over the globe with strong financial support from venture capital. Interestingly, the Boston Consulting Group report that while the many hundreds of small biotech companies only account for 3% of the drug industry's spending on R&D, they can lay claim to 67% of the current drugs in clinical trials. US biotechnology sales grew 20% in 2006 to $40 billion compared to 8% growth of traditional pharmaceutical sales to a level of $275 billion according to the consulting firm, IMS Health.

The complexity of biological drugs means that they are quite difficult to manufacture on a large scale but big pharma companies, such as Novartis, are now expanding their global manufacturing facilities rapidly to encompass the production of these large molecules.

Biologic drugs possibly offer the best hope for the treatment of diseases of the immune system such as multiple sclerosis, rheumatoid arthritis and lupus. These auto-immune diseases afflict some 23 million people in the US and impose a burden of some $100 billion on the healthcare system, being almost double the cost of cancer treatment.

13.3 Stem Cells

Stem cells are found, for example, in embryos and are the precursors to the formation of a diverse range of specialized cells of various tissues such as muscles and nerves. They also occur in adults and act as the repair system for cells in the body such as blood, skin and intestinal tissues, hence, the strong interest in the potential application of stem cells, as shown in Fig. 13.4, for therapeutic cell regeneration purposes.

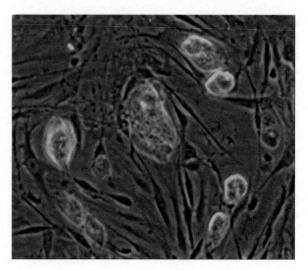

Fig. 13.4 Human stem cells
(Source: Wikimedia Commons)

Research based on the use of human embryonic stem cells has created some controversy. The ensuing debate has prompted authorities around the world to seek regulatory frameworks for stem cell research. However, recent research in Japan and the US has revealed that a so-called induced pluripotent stem cell (iPS) can be produced from adult skin cells. These cells were shown to closely resemble embryonic stem cells whereby brain, heart and other tissues could be made from these materials. This would indeed be a significant breakthrough if these iPS cells could be used for treating human diseases such as diabetes and Parkinson's and provide a solution to the embryonic stem cell ethical issue.

The recent discovery that cancers also have stem cells which are crucial to tumour growth has significant implications for drug development. There now appears to be good evidence that cancer stem cells are resistant to standard cancer chemotherapies which may explain the highly variable results. Early research indicates that new therapies that target cancer stem cells may be more effective. These encouraging results may lead to a whole new approach to anti-cancer drugs that could provide the breakthrough that has challenged researchers for decades.

13.4 Personalized Medicine

The often markedly different responses of patients to drug treatments, both positive and negative, are thought to be largely due to subtle but biologically very important differences in human gene structures, so-called genotypes. This has led to the concept of "designer drugs" or pharmacogenomics where the therapeutic treatment will be more closely tailored to the genotype of the individual patient.

An example of such a therapeutic strategy is that of the biologic drug, Herceptin, which is used to treat some forms of breast cancer. The use of this drug is based on the identification of the over expression of a protein receptor molecule called HER-2 in selected target patients. Another cancer drug developed by Novartis, called Gleevec, treats chronic myeloid leukaemia and is also a highly targeted drug which works by killing specific cancer cells whereas chemotherapy can kill both deranged and healthy cells. Pharmacogenomics tests that will predict individual responses are under development for drugs such as the breast cancer treatment, Tamoxifen and the lung cancer drug, Gefitinib.

Although personalized medicine is still very much in its infancy, it does hold quite some promise for the development of therapeutics that will be targeted to the specific genes that are involved in human diseases rather than the current block-buster strategy of "one drug fits all".

13.5 Genetic Testing

Genetic testing does not only have the potential for personalized medicine but also has the promise to determine the individual risk of developing ailments such as heart disease, cancer, osteoporosis and diabetes. The recent announcement of at least two companies, deCODE genetics based in Iceland and 23andMe, a Silicon Valley start-up funded by Google and Genetech, offering individual genome decoding for less than $1,000, is a step towards these ambitious goals.

Given that there are some 3 billion nucleotide letters in the human genome and that almost all of these are identical, a quantum innovation was required to achieve this fast genetic testing. The technology detects the small differences between individuals called single nucleotide polymorphisms (SNP's) of which there are some 10 million, rather than the whole genome. A microchip coated with millions of small beads which are embedded with bits of DNA that are complementary to the genome SNP's is the clever innovation of the genetic test.

However, although a very active field of medical research, a detailed understanding of how genetic variations relate to particular diseases and the interpretation of the decoded genome is currently lacking. Early research by deCODE genetics suggests that a gene called TCF7L2 may be linked to type 2 diabetes. This biotech company is using its insight into gene-based diseases to provide validated protein targets for the development of new therapeutic drugs.

A company called 454 Life Sciences Corporation recently sequenced the entire 3 billion letters of the genome of the Nobel prize winner, James Watson in two months. As a catalyst to further genomic innovation, the X Prize Foundation is now offering the Archon genomics prize of $10 million to the first team able to sequence 100 complete human genomes accurately in 10 days or less.

Another company called Helicos Bioscience has developed a machine that is capable of reading 1.3 billion DNA base pairs in about 1 hour. Helicos and other companies are targeting to develop equipment in the near future that will sequence a complete genome for only $1,000. These machines will generate terabytes of DNA data that will require advanced search technology to correlate these massive base pair sequences to human disease.

Clearly, this field of genetic research is advancing rapidly and will likely have a major impact on drug development and advanced therapeutic disease treatment in the near future, almost certainly leading to some exciting and disruptive innovation in the field of human health.

13.6 Immortal Medicine

The aging "baby-boomers" are triggering a heightened level of interest in the retardation of the human aging process. A number of biotech companies are focusing on the development of new drugs to increase longevity. Sirtris Pharmaceuticals, based in Cambridge in the US, has developed a formulation based on resveratrol, the "healthy" ingredient in red wine. Resveratrol is known to activate proteins called sirtuins which control glucose levels and improve insulin sensitivity which is potentially beneficial in terms of both aging and the treatment of type 2 diabetes. The Sirtris researchers have apparently discovered some novel, small-molecules drug candidates, so-called sirtuin super-stimulators, which are significantly more effective than resveratrol. If these new molecules are both effective and non-toxic, this would certainly be a disruptive innovation where the market opportunity for life extension drugs would seem to be also patentially immortal. A more radical approach to aging, so-called regenerative medicine, would be to use stem cells to grow spare tissues and organs that could be replaced as required.

Aging is another field of research which has attracted a prize to develop what is called the Methuselah mouse, and thereby stimulate innovation in the aging process. Aubrey de Grey is offering this prize for the development of a new strain of mouse that is either bred or genetically engineered and has a significantly extended lifespan. The translation of these mouse results to the human aging process will no doubt present some scientific challenges.

13.7 Cutting Edge Surgery

No one could have predicted that more than 50% of prostate surgical procedures in the US would now be carried out remotely by a surgeon using computer controlled robotic arms. The success of this disruptive technology is the result of combining haptic technology (computer-aided touch sensitivity) with micro (laparoscopic) surgery. The instruments are designed with seven degrees of motion that mimic the dexterity of the human hand and wrist.

Intuitive Surgical was granted FDA approval for their so-called da Vinci system, as shown in Fig. 13.5, for prostate surgery in May 2001. Like most new invasive technologies, early adoption by surgeons was slow but the first results in terms of reduced blood loss, lower risk of complications and faster regain of urinary and sexual function for prostate surgery have now overcome this early initial resistance. The

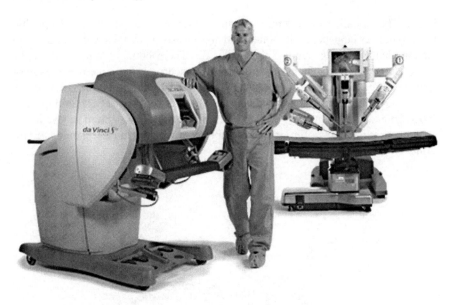

Fig. 13.5 Da Vinci robotic surgery
(Source: Intuitive Surgical Media photos, © 2009 Intuitive Surgical, Inc.)

success of this medical device technology is reflected in the astronomical growth in the stock price of Intuitive Surgical in the past few years with a current market capitalization of about $5 billion.

The applications of this innovative technology are now rapidly expanding into other surgical procedures such as hysterectomies and mitral valve repair. Further, the company has expanded into other markets beyond North America such as Asia, Australia, New Zealand and Europe. Interestingly, they have created a strong competitive position by extensive patent filing, early FDA approval, first mover on training surgeons and the hospital "prestige effect" of having such "state of the art" technology.

Researchers in Germany at the Institute of Robotics and Mechatronics believe that their new robotic-surgery system will soon be able to operate directly on a beating heart. This advanced technology creates a "virtually stationary image" whereby the surgeon can operate on a heart that appears to have stopped beating. In addition, this robotic surgery will use key-hole techniques that will greatly reduce the trauma associated with conventional open heart surgery.

All these innovative developments indicate that robotic surgery is poised to revolutionize the operating room of the future.

13.8 Razor Sharp Radiology

Another innovative company in the field of robotic medical devices is Accuray Inc., which has developed advanced technology for radio surgery and has been recognized as a healthcare Technology Pioneer for 2008 by the World Economic

Forum. The so-called CyberKnife system enables surgeons to accurately (within 0.5 mm) deliver large doses of radiation to non-invasively treat cancer tumours with minimal damage to surrounding healthy tissue. The robotic system, for example, enables surgeons to irradiate lung tumours and synchronize with the rise and fall of a patient's breathing. To date, more than 100 of the $4 million robotic radiotherapy systems have been sold and the company has an order backlog of $600 million. The CyberKnife, as shown in Fig. 13.6, can be considered as a quantum innovation in the field of radiotherapy offering considerable improvement in patient outcomes for certain types of cancer.

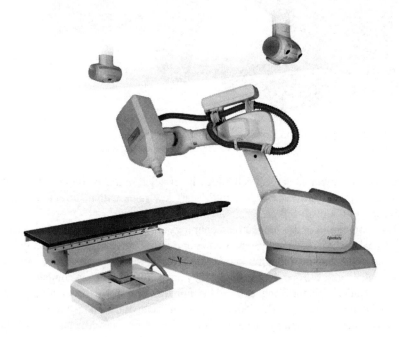

Fig. 13.6 CyberKnife radiotherapy
(Source: Accuracy)

13.9 Non-invasive Imaging

Innovation continues strongly in the development of advanced non-invasive technologies that provide a 3-dimensional view of damaged or diseased human tissues or organs. Modern medical scanning technologies include X-ray computed tomography (CT), magnetic resonance imaging (MRI), functional magnetic resonance imaging (fMRI), positron emission tomography and ultrasound.

Philips has developed a new CT scanner that rapidly produces high quality images including complete coverage of the heart and brain. The system is so sensitive that an image of the heart can be captured in just two beats while the X-ray radiation dosage is reduced by 80% compared to conventional technology.

Magnetic resonance imaging (MRI) makes use of radio waves to detect tiny signals from inside the body which is surrounded by a strong magnetic field. A computer turns these tiny signals into three-dimensional images. MRI is able to detect and distinguish between soft tissues in the body and is, therefore, a powerful diagnostic technique as shown in Fig. 13.7.

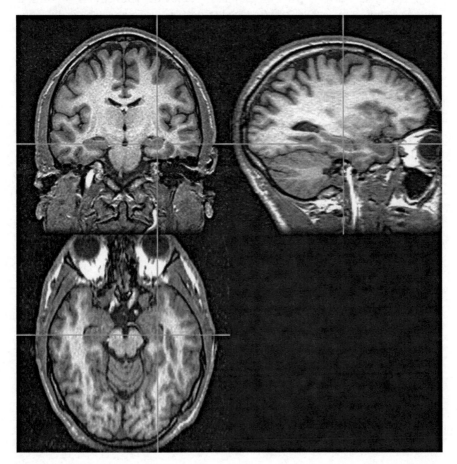

Fig. 13.7 MRI brain scan
(Source: Wikimedia Commons)

MRI is the method of choice for the diagnosis of many injuries and conditions including disorders of the brain, spine and joints. More recently, with advanced technology, imaging of the heart, blood vessels and abdomen has become common place.

Functional magnetic resonance imaging, fMRI, is a powerful new technique for measuring brain activity, which works by detecting the changes in blood oxygenation and flow that occur in response to neural activity. For example, when a brain area is more active, it consumes more oxygen and, to meet this increased demand, blood flow increases to the active area which is captured by the magnetic resonance imaging technology. Brain activation maps are produced showing which parts of the brain are involved in a particular mental process.

Positron emission tomography (PET) is a nuclear medicine medical imaging technique which produces a three-dimensional image of functional processes in the body. The system detects pairs of gamma rays emitted indirectly by a positron-emitting radioisotope, which is introduced into the body on a metabolically active molecule. Images of metabolic activity in space are then reconstructed by computer analysis.

In the future, many of these scanning technologies will be integrated to provide detailed 3-dimensional images of all the tissues and organs of the human body. In fact, CT and PET scanning have already been integrated providing a powerful new non-invasive cancer diagnostic tool.

Innovation in healthcare continues unabated with recent major advances in robotic surgery and proven benefits of rapid post-operative recovery. Non-invasive 3D body scanning technologies are routine and are becoming ever more powerful diagnostic tools. Although innovation appears to be stalling with new blockbuster drugs, exciting developments in DNA technology hold promise that the age of personalized medicine may be dawning. Stem cell technology is now advancing rapidly and human replacement parts may be on the horizon. The discovery of cancer stem cells offers an exciting new approach for the development of new and, possibly, more effective therapies.

Chapter 14
Nanotech Innovation

Miniaturization has been a powerful technological driving force for some decades with the electronic microchip industry as a familiar example. Gordon Moore predicted some 40 years ago that the number of transistors on a chip would double, as a result of incremental innovation, every 18 months to two years and "Moore's law" has proven to be remarkably accurate.

The term nanotechnology is employed for the creation and application of materials with particle sizes in the range 1–100 nm, a nanometer being one billionth (one thousand-millionth) of a metre. At this level of miniaturization, materials are in the form of small clusters of atomic particles and often exhibit physical and chemical properties quite different from larger particles of the same or similar composition. This can be exploited in novel devices and products that are beginning to achieve market penetration in various branches. Many new companies, often supported by venture capital, are adopting strategies that focus around developing nanotechnology for a wide variety of applications.

For example, the anti-bacterial property of minute particles of silver, has been one of the first applications of nano-materials. Nano-silver is now quite widely applied and can now be found in bandages, food storage containers, shoe liners, sportswear and toilets. Minute particles of titanium dioxide are used to make transparent UV filtering sunscreens and self-cleaning surface coatings.

14.1 Nano-charged Batteries

Perhaps one of the most exciting recent developments in this field is a nano-material discovered by Professor Chiang and co-workers at the Massachusetts Institute of Technology (MIT) in the US that has led to a new generation of Li-ion batteries. Chiang developed a new nano-particle electrode material called lithium iron phosphate which has also been modified with trace metals. This new material exhibits electrical properties that enable lithium-ion batteries to be produced with double the power density and much faster recharging than current cobalt-based lithium-ion cells.

I.E. Maxwell, *Managing Sustainable Innovation*,
DOI 10.1007/978-0-387-87581-1_14, © 2009 by Ian E. Maxwell

Electricity is generated in these batteries when lithium ions shuttle between two electrodes and electrons travel through an external circuit. Chiang's research revealed that as lithium ions moved in and out of an electrode, the crystalline structure of the material changed and the battery performance deteriorated. However, when the particles of lithium iron phosphate are small enough and the electrode is modified through the addition of other metals, the crystalline structure is largely retained. As a result, the lithium ions can migrate faster without degrading the electrode material. In addition, the modified material charged and discharged faster than ordinary lithium iron phosphate and also had a longer useful lifetime.

These discoveries led to the formation of A123 Systems in 2001, which licensed this nano-phosphate technology from MIT. To date, A123 has raised $250 million in funding from "Silicon Valley" venture capital giants such as Sequoia Capital and major strategic investors such as GE, Duracell (owned by Proctor & Gamble) and Qualcomm to commercialize this second generation lithium-ion battery (Fig. 14.1).

Fig. 14.1 The GM volt electric car powered by A123 lithium – ion batteries (Source: Wikimedia commons)

Interestingly, A123 has quietly perfected the technology and built wholly owned manufacturing facilities in China to produce the first of these new batteries for the electric power tool multinational, Black & Decker, which will consume their entire first year of production. The high performance of these new generation batteries also opens the path for a major potential application in both hybrid and plug-in electric cars.

14.2 Nano-flash Memory

Nanotechnology plays a key role in the rapidly advancing field of memory storage devices for application in computers, memory cards, USB drives, MP3 players, digital cameras and the new generation of smart mobile phones such as the Apple iPhone. Flash memory is the most in demand as this is a so-called non-volatile computer memory which retains all the stored information even when there is no power to the device.

The Japanese giant, Samsung, recently stated that there is currently "exploding demand" for flash memory as a storage medium in a range of applications. The race is raging among the big players such as Intel, Micron, Samsung, Toshiba and SanDisk to develop greater flash storage capacity. The most advanced systems currently achieve 128 GB of memory, making flash technology a rival to conventional hard drives. To achieve such high levels of storage, these devices are miniaturizing to well below 100 nm with Toshiba, for example, recently announcing plans to use 30 nm technology. In fact, the rapid rate of miniaturization of flash memory appears to be another example of Moore's law as shown in Fig. 14.2.

Fig. 14.2 Moore's law for flash memory miniaturization (Redrawn from Wikimedia commons)

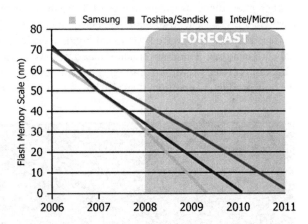

As in the case of computer chips, flash memory will reach a physical limit at about 20 nm after which, they will likely resort to 3D stacking to further increase storage capacity. Alternatively, a totally new and disruptive storage technology may emerge and drive down a new Moore's law curve.

14.3 Nano Transistor Gates

The microelectronic industry which has been at the nano level for some time is now struggling to overcome the challenges of the super-small, where the component parts become a cluster of atoms as in transistor gates. The modern transistor uses a small voltage at a place called a gate to regulate the flow of current through the rest of the device. It is this switching of current that forms the basis of the computing process deploying the zeros and ones of binary arithmetic. These gates, which are made of silicon, need to be electrically insulated, which is achieved by exposing them to pure oxygen and creating a thin surface layer of silicon dioxide.

However, as transistors have become even smaller, this silicon dioxide layer has been reduced to only a few atoms thick; the consequent weakening of the insulator properties resulting in current leakage and power loss.

To solve this problem, researchers at Intel have screened a wide range of alternative materials and discovered that hafnium oxide has excellent gate insulating properties. Although the microelectronic manufacturing process is more complex, the new Intel Penryn chips, which have about a billion transistors, make use of hafnium oxide to reduce power loss in the gates.

14.4 Carbon Nano-tubes

Carbon nano-tubes, as shown in Fig. 14.3, are the strongest and stiffest materials on earth, in terms of tensile strength and elastic modulus respectively.

This strength results from chemical bonds formed directly between the individual carbon atoms. These novel nano-materials have already been used as composite fibres in polymers to improve the mechanical, thermal and electrical properties of the bulk product. In addition, they also have other unique properties due to their nano

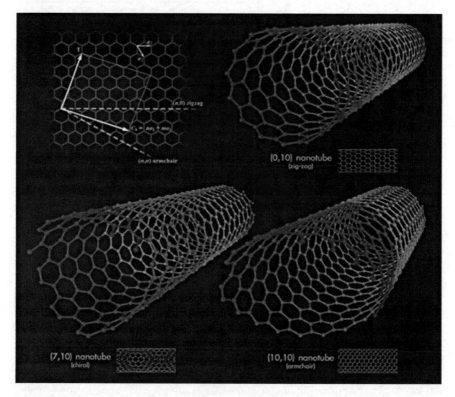

Fig. 14.3 Carbon nano-tubes (Source: Wikimedia commons)

dimensions that make them ideal components of electrical circuits, Although carbon nano-tubes are still very expensive to manufacture, which is a current limitation to widespread application of this novel material, their semi-conductor properties are beginning to lead to applications in micro-electronics. The US company, Nantero, is producing RAM memory chips based on thin films of carbon nano-tubes, while at the University of Illinois, researchers have succeeded in making flexible computer chips, with many potential applications, from carbon nano-tubes supported on plastic film.

14.5 Nano-drugs

Designing effective drugs is challenging and complex since they not only have to be effective for the disease but they also have to be robust enough to defeat natural human defences and reach the part of the body to be treated.

A new approach to drugs is based on a phenomenon called RNA interference (RNAi). RNA is the molecule in the body that carries the message from DNA to the places in the cell where proteins are made. The RNAi drug works by blocking these molecular messengers which are producing proteins that are responsible for a disease such as a cancer tumour. In fact, the drug itself is also a type of RNA molecule that is able to pair with the disease-causing RNA messenger and thereby inhibit its protein production function.

However, the challenge has been to develop an RNAi molecule that is sufficiently robust to penetrate into cells to perform their therapeutic function. Researchers Siwen Hu and Timothy Triche, at the Children's Hospital in Los Angeles, together with Mark Davis from the California Institute of Technology appear to have overcome this problem by wrapping the RNAi inside a nano-particle made from a combination of biodegradable polymeric materials. After the nano-particle has penetrated the cell wall of a cancer tumour, the acidic environment inside dissolves the particle releasing the RNAi drug molecule.

Animal testing of these nano-particle RNAi drugs has to date shown very promising results for retarding or even terminating the growth of particular cancer tumours. These promising results could lead to broader applications of nano-particles for the delivery of bio-molecule based drugs in the future.

14.6 Nano-biopolymers

Medical researchers at MIT in the US and at the University of Hong Kong in China have developed nano-fibres made from small biodegradable protein structures. These novel materials self-assemble from certain peptide (the sub-units of proteins) sequences when immersed in salt solutions.

Surgeons are already excited about this new bio-polymeric material that shows great promise to dramatically stop living tissue bleeding and therefore has potential applications in the fields of eye, gastrointestinal and brain surgery.

14.7 Nanotech Tipping Point?

While there continue to be fascinating scientific and technological developments in the field of nanotechnology, the initial promise of a revolution in materials science does not yet appear to have been realized. In addition, some health researchers have recently raised some concerns about the potential toxicity of nano-materials but the field and applications are so broad, this will likely only be addressed on a case-by-case basis.

Clearly, in some major application areas such as batteries, flash memory and computer chips, and some consumer personal-care products, nanotechnology has already made an impact. Perhaps a tipping point for nanotechnology innovation, with more general penetration, will indeed emerge in the near future.

Chapter 15
Prize Innovation

The offer of substantial prizes for achievements in specific areas can provide a powerful stimulus to innovation. A competition launched in the 17th century, for example, resulted in the creation of a method to accurately estimate longitude. This innovation business model has recently been reinvigorated with a wide range of new prizes being offered for achieving well defined and, often, very challenging technical goals. Many of these prizes target technology solutions to major global issues.

15.1 X-PRIZES

Bodies offering prizes include both private and governmental organizations. One of the largest is the X PRIZE Foundation that "creates and manages prizes that drive innovators to solve some of the greatest challenges facing the world today". This novel foundation, which was founded by Dr Peter Diamandis, is a non-profit, educational organization which stimulates competition to create innovative breakthroughs for the benefit of mankind. Notable Google is a partner of the foundation and Larry Page (co-founder of Google) is a member of their so-called vision circle.

15.2 Space Technology

The first major prize offered by the X Prize Foundation, the $10 million Ansari X PRIZE, was a space competition for the first non-government organization to launch a reusable manned spacecraft into space twice within two weeks. The prize was won on October 4, 2004, by the Tier One project designed by Burt Rutan and financed by Microsoft co-founder, Paul Allen, using the experimental spaceplane, SpaceShipOne. It is estimated that more than $100 million was invested in new technologies in pursuit of the prize. The success of this innovation competition has led to the concept of SpaceShipTwo (SS2) which is an innovative, low-cost, commercial suborbital plane.

I.E. Maxwell, *Managing Sustainable Innovation*,
DOI 10.1007/978-0-387-87581-1_15, © 2009 by Ian E. Maxwell

Virgin Galactic is marketing and operating the vehicles and hopes to become the first company to provide commercial suborbital space flights for private citizens. The company is planning the first public flight before 2009 and is now taking bookings at $200,000 per seat. Flights will take about $2\frac{1}{2}$ hours and SS2 will fly just outside of the Earth's atmosphere where tourists will spend a few minutes floating in space before the ship returns back to the Earth's atmosphere. SS2 will be launched from its mother ship, WhiteKnightTwo (WK2), which will have the same interior as the SS2 and will be used to help train passengers during a three-day orientation period before launch.

In September 2007 the Google Lunar X PRIZE was announced. This is a $30 million international competition to safely land a robot on the surface of the moon by 2012, travel 500 meters over the lunar surface, and send images and data back to Earth. Competitors must be at least 90% privately funded and the first team to land on the Moon and complete the mission objectives will be awarded $20 million. The second team to do so will receive $5 million and a further $5million will be awarded in bonus prizes.

Another space technology contest is the Northrop Grumman Lunar Lander Challenge. This is designed to accelerate commercial technological developments supporting the birth of a new generation of Lunar Landers, capable of ferrying payloads or people back and forth between lunar orbit and the lunar surface. Such a vehicle would have direct application to NASA's space exploration goals as well as the personal spaceflight industry, and might also find application in delivering the Lunar X Prize robot to its destination. Additionally, the challenge will help industry develop the operational capacity to launch quick turnaround vertical take-off and landing vehicles, which will be of significant use to the commercial launch market.

15.3 Human Health

The second X PRIZE, the Archon X PRIZE also of $10 million, was announced in October 2006 by the Foundation. The prize is $10 million for the first nongovernmental organization to sequence the complete genomes of 100 humans in 10 days' time. The use of personal genetic information to predict disease susceptibility and guide proactive care has the power to transform our entire healthcare system.

Hence, this is a very exciting time in genomics where scientists are on the brink of discovering the genetic factors in diabetes, heart disease, common cancers, high blood pressure, asthma, mental illness and virtually any disease that tends to run in families. Finding the genetic factors that predispose someone to disease, and how they are likely to respond to different treatments may be determined not by one gene but by many genes interacting with each other. Combing through this complicated genetic map is expensive and time consuming.

It currently costs millions of dollars and takes many months to sequence an individual genome. The Archon Genomics X-PRIZE is aimed at greatly reducing the cost and increasing the speed of human genome sequencing such that the promise of personalized medicine can be realized.

In the field of life sciences, a Cancer X PRIZE Suite is being explored. The intention is to stimulate innovation in directions that are perpendicular to the existing multi-billion dollar research programs currently funded by large pharmaceutical companies. The prize will include incentives covering all cancer prevention, diagnosis and therapy. Another life science-related potential project being explored by the foundation is the Human Longevity X PRIZE which is aimed at extending the human lifespan and improving the quality of life and health in old age. This balance is considered essential since quality of life continues to decrease if people are not healthy as they grow older. In addition, the number of healthcare resources consumed will increase dramatically. Only by a parallel increase in the quality of life can a radical breakthrough in human longevity be achieved.

The New Scientist magazine recently posed the question as to whether cash prizes should be used to promote the development of cheap drugs. Existing medical prizes include the Prize4Life, the Archon X Prize, the M prize and the Grainger challenge. A US senator, Bernie Sanders, has proposed an ambitious bill called the "Medical Innovation Prize Fund" which he believes would displace the monopolies for new drugs in the US by providing more than $30 billion a year in cash prizes for innovations that improve health. Such a drastic departure from the current, largely market driven model of health innovation would likely be highly challenging for government organizations to manage the complexity and risk of drug development effectively.

15.4 Transportation

The Progressive Automotive X PRIZE, promises a prize to the first non-governmental organization to create, market, and produce in significant quantities an automobile capable of travelling at least 100 miles on 1 gallon of gasoline. The independent and technology-neutral competition is open to teams from around the world that can design, build and bring to market super efficient vehicles that people want to buy, and that meet market needs for price, size, capability, safety and performance. To date, more than 60 teams from nine countries have signed a Letter of Intent to compete for a share of the prize purse and global publicity.

As a stimulus to innovation in the field of biofuels, a prize is being developed for technology which does not compete with food crops, can be produced on a small scale, and is easily transported. A Village Utility X PRIZE is under review to use the power of competition to develop models that enable communities in the developing world to uplift their living standards and break the cycle of global poverty. The global competition would likely leverage technology-based innovation to develop more effective ways to deliver power, water and connectivity to communities in need in the developing world. This competition will reward invention of such a device and/or ways to distribute that technology.

15.5 Mobile Phone Software

Google has recently announced a total of $10 million in prizes for software development related to their mobile phone platform called Android. The contest has been launched under the banner "Android Developer Challenge" and the prizes range from $25,000 to $275,000. Google has released a tool kit for developers working on its new platform. Android mobile software will be offered free to mobile phone manufacturers and Google believes that the propagation of this software platform will enhance its advertising and services businesses. Motorola, Samsung Electronics, HTC and LG Electronics have all agreed to use Android in some of their phones. This new software platform will compete directly with mobile operating systems offered by Microsoft, Palm, Research in Motion and Symbian (now owned by Nokia Corporation).

This is an interesting example of the combined use of prize innovation, open innovation and business model innovation to rapidly, and likely at relatively low cost, develop a new product and then launch it in an existing market. Such novel and dramatic developments in innovation modes will pose major challenges to established players in these market segments.

15.6 Climate Change

British billionaire entrepreneur, Richard Branson has offered a $25 million prize to anyone who can come up with a way to tackle global climate change by removing at least a billion tons of carbon dioxide a year from the Earth's atmosphere.

Former US Vice President, Al Gore, will serve as a judge in the contest known as the Virgin Earth Challenge which is targeted to spur scientific innovation without distracting from more practical steps people can take to battle global warming.

Although scientists are working on technologies to capture carbon dioxide and other greenhouse gases at power plants and other industrial sources, strategies to remove gases already released into the atmosphere are only at a very early stage of development. Perhaps, the most promising approach to this challenge will be to develop genetically modified biological systems that are capable of converting carbon dioxide together with sunlight into organic materials that are suitable feedstock for conversion into biofuels or bulk industrial chemicals.

The winner of the contest must devise a plan to remove greenhouse gases from the atmosphere without creating adverse effects. A further challenge is that the first $5 million will be paid up-front and the remainder of the money will be paid only after the program has worked successfully for 10 years. The backers of this prize have referred repeatedly to the November, 2007 report of the Intergovernmental Panel on Climate Change (IPCC) made up of hundreds of scientists from 113 countries, which concluded that human activity is warming the planet at a potentially disastrous and irreversible rate.

15.7 Robotic Cars

The DARPA Grand Challenge is a prize aimed at advancing robotic cars which, until recently, struggled to make their way around even basic obstacles such as large rocks and potholes in the road, unable to mimic what a human can do behind the wheel. This challenge event requires teams to build an autonomous vehicle capable of driving in traffic, performing complex manoeuvres such as merging, passing, parking and negotiating intersections. An autonomous ground vehicle is a vehicle that navigates and drives entirely on its own with no human driver and no remote control. Through the use of various sensors and positioning systems, the vehicle determines all the characteristics of its environment required to enable it to carry out the task it has been assigned.

Partly due to the DARPA challenge, the new generation of robotic cars can squeeze into parking places and almost display the flair of a London taxi driver when merging into traffic. This improvement in autonomous vehicle technology is such that the US defence department hopes a third of its ground vehicles will be robotic by 2015. The total DARPA prize money is $3.5 million, of which $2 million goes to the vehicle best able to negotiate its way around a former air force base in southern California, with $1 million and $500,000 for second and third places.

The X-PRIZE approach to innovation does seem to be working, judging by the interest in these events to date. Perhaps, the most important aspect of the foundation is that they pose very demanding technical challenges in areas where the commercial benefits are often not apparent, at least in the short term. Hence, the X PRIZE Foundation is contributing to the high risk disruptive mode of innovation, generating innovative breakthroughs in new and exciting areas. The foundation plans to launch ten new prizes over the next five years with a combined purse amount of approximately $100 million. New prizes will focus on pushing the limits of what is currently possible, and accelerating the rate of positive change, all for the benefit of humanity. In order to meet these goals, the X PRIZE Foundation has a dedicated prize development team who will build competitions that capture the public imagination and inspire results. Future prizes are being proposed in the fields of education, energy and environment, exploration, global entrepreneurship and life sciences.

Chapter 16
Sustainable Innovation

16.1 Innovation Acceleration

The rate of innovation is expected to increase rapidly as knowledge grows exponentially and the global research expenditure on science and technology proliferates. The large numbers of scientists and engineers graduating from universities in the developing countries such as China and India will further reinforce this trend.

As previously discussed, it would appear that we are moving rapidly towards the sixth innovation wave of the Schumpeter theory. Indeed, there is good evidence to suggest that this wave may be driven by the current pace of innovation in the fields of renewable energy, clean technology, genomic developments in biotechnology and new materials emerging from nano-technology as shown in Fig. 16.1.

This innovation acceleration will create a new paradigm in which only nimble companies will likely achieve sustainability in a highly competitive, global knowledge driven economy.

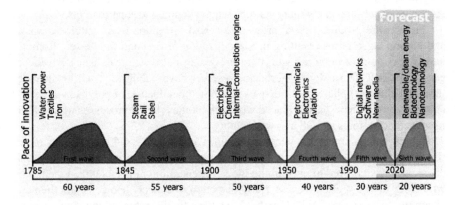

Fig. 16.1 The sixth innovation wave (Author's drawing)

I.E. Maxwell, *Managing Sustainable Innovation*,
DOI 10.1007/978-0-387-87581-1_16, © 2009 by Ian E. Maxwell

16.2 Future Scenarios

The following scenarios are intended to paint a possible future within a few decades driven by accelerating innovation and assuming no major global political upheavals. Although these scenarios are highly speculative, they are intended to inspire a vision of the huge potential benefits that innovation could provide, not only in terms of wealth creation but, even more importantly, enhance human well-being all over the world.

In the not too distant future, major advances will be made in renewable energy with solar, geothermal and wind power developments driving down cost curves such that global energy costs could potentially reach a turning point and start decreasing in real terms. In addition, the strong shift to renewable energy and breakthroughs in carbon conversion technologies have curbed and even lowered carbon dioxide levels, avoiding a climate change crisis of global proportions.

A number of countries such as Denmark, Iceland, New Zealand, the Arab Emirates and some southern states of the US have achieved close to 100% power generation from renewable sources. Zero carbon emission cities have become more globally widespread following the lead and overwhelming success of the city of Masdar in the Arab Emirates.

Smart buildings have incorporated thin-film solar energy technology into the exterior architecture dramatically reducing energy consumption. This low cost and highly efficient thin-film solar technology is also being widely used to generate home energy needs with excess electricity being fed into the national grids. The home-distributed electricity production has resulted in the closure of existing coal-fired power stations in most countries around the world.

The latest generation of batteries based on nanotechnology with rapid charging rates and high power density has revolutionized the storage of solar and wind power enabling these technologies to provide a continuous source of electricity. Plug-in electric vehicles are now the dominant private means of transport and most major cities only allow zero emission vehicles within the city limits. The recharging of plug-in vehicles occurs overnight from batteries that have been charged from home solar roof panels and at charging stations while shopping at supermarkets.

Biofuels are produced on a large scale across the globe from cellulosic waste and marine algae farms resulting in a stabilization of fuel and food costs. Remote natural gas fields around the world are producing petrochemicals using advanced gas to liquids (GTL) and global crude oil reserves have stabilized. Traditional crude oil based chemical plants previously used for the manufacture of polymers and speciality chemicals have been replaced with new biomass based processes which offer improved economics as well as sustainability.

Robotic microsurgery has become the norm and has reversed the previous rapid rise in surgical procedure costs. Individual gene testing has become routine and physicians have moved to prescribing the new generation of personalized medicine with close to 100% effectiveness. Early detection of cancer stem cells and the new generation of selective RNA blocking drugs have finally achieved the long awaited breakthrough in cancer therapy.

Stem cell technology has also become a routine procedure for organ transplants eliminating waiting times, removing rejection side effects and lowering costs. Genetic engineering has provided a cure for all gene-based diseases and a global ethics code is in force to manage the rapidly emerging businesses based on new life and plant forms created from synthetic genomes.

New generations of genetically modified plants have achieved huge gains in productivity for both biofuel and food production. Basic food costs have been driven down to a price point whereby starvation has almost been eliminated on the planet.

Smart mobile web enabled devices provide TV coverage, movies, games, 3D animation, global navigation, personal health records and free advanced computing applications through touch screen and voice interaction. Household appliances are now connected to the web and can be controlled from these devices.

China has become the largest global economy and has achieved a position among the top five countries in the world innovation rankings together with India. Low cost innovation has created a paradigm shift with successful companies effectively managing global innovation value chains.

Microeconomics has gradually created sustainable small scale business solutions further reducing poverty in underdeveloped countries. Technology leapfrogging and rapid diffusion have enabled developing countries to enjoy high GDP growth rates and decrease the wealth gap with developed countries.

The aged baby boomers in the developed world are enjoying healthier, longer and more active lives due to advanced protein based anti-aging treatments, stem cell organ replacements, individual gene based nutritional diets and household robotic support systems.

The first Mars X prize has been presented to the team that landed on Mars and carried out space walks including geological exploration.

16.3 Sustainable Innovation

The development of vibrant innovation infrastructures at both the company and country level will be vital to achieve sustainable financial performance and GDP growth, respectively. Innovation leadership will need to be driven top down by company senior management to ensure that this has the level of priority required needed throughout the organization to succeed. Governments will also need to show strong leadership, and ensure that well-directed policies are implemented to strengthen the science and technology foundation as well as the innovation infrastructure of their countries. Smaller countries with modest science and technology budgets will have to make some hard choices as to the areas where they will focus their scarce resources to be able to compete in the global arena in both the short and longer term.

Low cost innovation emerging from rapidly developing economies such as China and India will create a whole new level of global competition posing significant challenges for developed countries with much higher cost structures. Companies will need to adopt a global perspective with regard to the optimization of the innovation value chain.

All of the above, together with the megatrend of innovation acceleration, will present major challenges, and the companies and governments that are able to demonstrate the leadership to embrace these dynamics will flourish and enjoy sustained growth in the new global economy.

Innovation will not only be the driver for global growth in the future but will also have a profound impact in providing potential solutions to some of the most challenging issues that currently face the world such as climate change, environmental pollution, fossil fuel shortages, third world poverty, rising healthcare costs, massive urbanization and aging populations.

Book Sources

The author would like to gratefully acknowledge the many high quality articles from the sources given below that have provided valuable research material for writing this book.

Magazines

Economist
Business Week
Newsweek
Time Magazine
New Scientist
Technology Review (MIT)
Forbes Magazine
Harvard Business Review

Newspapers

New York Times
Herald Tribune
China Daily
Beijing Daily
New Zealand Herald

Websites and Reports

http://knowledge.wharton
www.Earth2Tech
www.demos.co.uk

www.RenewableEnergyWorld.com
www.xprize.org
www.greentechmedia.com

White Papers

OECD Country Innovation Reports
Shell Technology Report
McKinsey Quarterly Reports
Demos (UK) reports on China, South Korea and India
Venture Capital Industry Report, Dow Jones, 2007

Books

"Open Innovation: The New Imperative for Creating and Profiting from Technology" by Henry William Chesbrough, Havard Business School Press, 2005
"Open Business Models: How to Thrive in the New Innovation Landscape" by Henry William Chesbrough, Havard Business School Press, 2006
"Innovation: The Five Disciplines for Creating What Customers Want" by Curtis R. Carlson and William W. Wilmot, Crown Business, 2006
"The Myths of Innovation" by Scott Berkun, O'Reilly Media, 2007
"Innovation Nation" by John Kao, Free Press, 2007
"The Innovators Solution" by Clayton Christensen and Michael Raynor, Havard Business School Press, 2003
"The Innovators Dilemma" by Clayton Christensen, Collins Business Essentials, 2003
"The Business of Healthcare Innovation" edited by Robert Burns, Cambridge University Press, 2005

Index

NOTE: The letter '*f*' following the locators refers to figures.